A Layman's Guide to Protestant Theology

REVISED EDITION

A LAYMAN'S GUIDE TO

Protestant Theology

REVISED EDITION

by William Hordern

MACMILLAN PUBLISHING CO., INC.

NEW YORK

COLLIER MACMILLAN PUBLISHERS

LONDON

TO MY WIFE

Acknowledgments

In a book of this nature, it is impossible to make adequate acknowledgment of all the sources that one has used. Inasmuch as I am trying to interpret theology for the lay or non-technical reader, I feel that extensive footnotes would be a hindrance. The section "Suggestions for Further Reading" is in no way a complete bibliography of the sources upon which I have drawn. It is a compilation of works that I believe will interest the layman. I am, of course, indebted to a host of authors too numerous to mention here.

A word of special gratitude must be expressed to William Hubben, editor of *Friends Intelligencer*. Early in 1953 he asked me to write a series of articles on modern theologians. The work on this series was an important factor in my decision to write a book on the subject, and many passages of this book originally appeared in those articles.

In the fall of 1953 I had the opportunity of giving large sections of this material before the Adult Forum of the Swarthmore Friends Meeting. This alert and intelligent audience gave me valuable aid by pointing out where I was vague or had failed to make my point.

I should like to extend my thanks to the Board of Managers of Swarthmore College for the leave of absence which made the writing of this book possible.

Last, but not least, I must express gratitude to my students. Five years at Swarthmore College have taught me much about presenting theological issues to an interested but critical laity.

W.H.

Contents

Preface to Revised Edition

When the first edition of this book appeared in 1955 I felt deeply that there was a need for a book that could introduce concerned laymen to contemporary theological discussion. The response to that volume proved that many laymen shared my concern. It is evident that laymen are ready to wrestle with theological debate.

Contary to many popular ideas, theology is not a static subject. Theologians are forced continually to relate the Christian faith to a changing world. As a result, it has been evident for some time that the original edition of *A Layman's Guide to Protestant Theology* had become dated. When, however, I undertook the task of revision it proved to be extremely difficult. How can one do justice to the manifold developments in theology since this book first appeared? In the first edition I was keenly aware that I was open to criticism for leaving out certain theological thinkers. But, in a book of this size, one cannot treat all of the significant theological trends. Although this revised edition is larger than the original, it is even more open to criticism because there are so many more theological currents today. Therefore, the reader is warned that this book is by no means a complete introduction to modern theology. If, however, it serves its purpose of stimulating the interested layman, he will go on with further reading to fill in the gaps that I have left.

W.H.

Introduction

This book arises from my conviction that there is a need for the Protestant laity to do more creative thinking about theology. But where is the layman to start? If he picks up a theological book he is likely to find himself baffled by terms that he cannot understand. Theology is as inaccessible to him as one of Einstein's treatises on relativity. Like every other science, theology has its technical terminology, its jargon. What this book tries to do is to introduce the layman to this field of thought in terms that he can understand. We shall use many technical terms, but when we do we shall try to define them.

First, we had better say why theology is necessary. This is by no means immediately apparent even to the devoted layman. J. P. Williams quotes a minister as saying: "I love flowers, but I hate botany; I love religion, but I hate theology." This attitude is widespread and is often based upon good reasons. Theology can become dull or even unchristian. But the answer to poor theology must be good theology, not no theology. We can see why this is so if we analyze what theology is.

"Theology" comes from two Greek words: *Theos,*

meaning God, and *logos*, meaning word or rational thought. Therefore theology is a word or rational thought about God. The word "God" cannot be defined exactly, but it is normally used to represent whatever is believed to be the Ultimate, the Source of everything else, the highest of values, the Source of all other values. God is that which is deemed worthy of being the goal and purpose of life. In light of this, it is almost self-evident that no man can live without theology.

Frequently someone says: "Why bother with theology? The theologians waste their time debating unimportant issues." Let us examine this statement. Why are these issues deemed unimportant? Obviously, the objector has in mind some concept of highest value by which he judges the arguments of theologians valueless. He has a theological position, a belief about the nature of God, which leads him to judge as unimportant the arguments of theologians. In short, even this attack upon theology is a theological attack.

Often we hear people say that it is not what a man believes, it is what he does that is important. This is a half-truth, but like all half-truths it is dangerous. It is half true because, from the Christian viewpoint, theological thinking is not an end in itself. Christianity is to be lived; it is to issue in action; as long as it remains merely thought it is unchristian and futile. But it is a *half*-truth because whatever a man does depends upon what he thinks and what he holds of ultimate value. When the so-called practical man is faced with the problem of deciding how to act in a given situation, he must have some implicit idea of what ends he wishes to obtain, what values ought to be gained from the solution. Furthermore, he must have some concept of the best means of achieving those values. All of this is theology, whether it be implicit or explicit.

The cliché "It's not what a man thinks but what he does that counts" seemed plausible as long as the great majority of men in our culture had a Christian scale of values. But we live in a world where precisely that scale of values is threatened and questioned. The moral ideals that seemed self-evident truths to our fathers have become problems for our day. Both Communists and Nazis have recognized that there is no simple distinction between what a man believes and what he does. As a result, they put great emphasis upon propaganda, the concerted attempt to change what men think. They knew that if they could change the thoughts of men about the ultimate nature of things and ultimate values, they could change the actions of men. Christian theology is nothing more nor less than the attempt to change the thinking of men so that they will act as Christians.

Because we live in a time when the ultimate meaning of life is questioned, we can no longer dodge such questions. A few years ago men thought that they could ignore ultimate questions and get along with the job of making this world a better place. Education, science, and technology could, they believed, solve all of our problems. But, as Dr. N. M. Pusey, president of Harvard University, pointed out in his already famous address to the Harvard Divinity

School, you do not get rid of these ultimate questions by pretending that they are not there. If you ignore them, they rise in perverted and distorted forms to mock you. Dr. Pusey's point is illustrated by totalitarianism, which arises when men can see nothing more ultimate than their state or economic class.

The attempt to think about God leads immediately to a host of related questions which are included under the term "theology." First, there is the question of man's relation to God, the Ultimate Source of things, including what he deems to be good. Thus we must ask about revelation; that is, How does man know what God is like? Can God be discovered by the same methods that discover scientific truth, or must God himself give some revelation of his nature to man? If God must reveal himself, where and how is he revealed?

This leads to the concept of sin. Sin occurs when man is out of harmony with the Source of his being and when he betrays his highest values. It is interesting to notice that even an ostensibly atheistic system, like that of Communism, cannot escape the problem of sin. Those who betray what the Communist believes to be the highest values are not called "sinners"; but they are called "Trotskyists," "Wall Street minions," "warmongers," "capitalist imperialists," and so on.

The question of sin leads to the question of salvation. Salvation occurs when a man, in some sense, overcomes the separation between himself and the Source of his being and when he becomes loyal to the highest values. How does man achieve salvation?

How does he overcome sin? Why does man sin in the first place? Why does man fail to achieve the highest values? Does he fall into sin naturally? Can he overcome sin and remain true to the highest that he knows by trying hard, or does he need help from beyond himself? Even the man who says that it is not what you believe but what you do that counts must have some answer, implicit or explicit, to these questions before he can act in any situation.

Behind these lie still more questions. How can men best organize themselves to work together for good? That is, what about the Church? Where is everything leading us? Where are we going? For what can we hope? Is this life, the history of man on this planet, the sum total of our opportunity to know the Highest, or is there a life and realm beyond this world in which our values will continue to their fulfillment? Such questions deal with what theologians call "eschatology."

So viewed, there is no escaping theological questions. We simply do not have the alternative of theology or no theology. Our alternatives are either to have a well thought-out theology, a theology which has passed the test of critical thought, or to have a hodgepodge theology of unexamined concepts, prejudices, and feelings. One of the weaknesses of Protestantism today is that so few Protestants know what they believe or why. This is a mistake that is seldom made by the Communist. The Communist party does a very thorough job of training its devotees. No half-hearted, half-thought-out religion can stand before the militant discipline of Communism. But we must not suppose that theology is made necessary by the threat of Communism. The Communist threat simply illustrates a basic fact about life.

The events of the twentieth century have led to a rebirth of Protestant theology. Men are once again wrestling with the ultimate questions of life and are trying to find the Christian answers. I hope that this book will help the layman to discover what is going on in theology. This book is not a complete picture; it is an introduction. It ought to lead the reader to further reading and certainly to further thought. The reader may or may not accept one of the theological positions to be described; but the book will have fulfilled its purpose if it helps the reader to work out his own theological position against the background of modern thought.

There are many ways in which one might introduce the layman to modern theology. One of the most obvious would be to discuss certain topics, such as sin, God, salvation, and give various interpretations of each. I believe that such a method would confuse rather than illuminate. Theology has to hang together; it develops into systems of thought in which the answer given to one question throws light upon the next. I have chosen, therefore, to present modern theology by examining various schools of thought. By this means we can illustrate the way in which each of the various systems forms an organic whole.

While this method is, I believe, the most desirable, it has certain shortcomings, and we must emphasize them. In the first place, as someone has said, "All labels are libels." There is always some injustice involved in putting a man into a school of thought. It too quickly identifies him with certain points of view which he may, in fact, repudiate. There is usually some individuality or originality about every thinker that is lost when you treat him as a member of a a school of thought. We have tried to bring out individual differences as far as possible, but the reader must realize that this is a weakness of our method that cannot be completely overcome. In a book that intends to be an introduction only, that is a price that perhaps has to be paid.

A second difficulty is that we are continually tempted to overemphasize the differences in viewpoint and to obscure the areas of agreement. We make a school's position clear by distinguishing it from another school. Furthermore, to list all the points of agreement would lead to wearisome repetition. Again, the reader must recall this limitation.

A third difficulty is that if we present theology in terms of modern schools of thought, we find that there are certain important thinkers who are mentioned only in passing and others who are ignored. The question of which theologians should be used to represent a school of thought is, of course, a matter of individual judgment. I cannot expect that everyone will agree with my particular choices.

Although our purpose is to introduce the reader to modern developments in theology, we have to begin with history. The problems which confront us today did not leap suddenly into life during the twentieth century. They were generated by our past and cannot be understood apart from it. We do not have the space to treat the history of Western thought adequately, but we have devoted two chapters to a quick summary of some of the most important elements of its background.

A Layman's Guide to Protestant Theology

REVISED EDITION

The Growth of Orthodoxy

It is almost impossible to use the term "orthodoxy" without stirring emotions. There are people who hate the thought of being unorthodox. For them orthodoxy, whether in politics, religion, or table manners, is the first necessity of life. To others, it is the most deplorable state into which a man can fall. It is equivalent to being stale, unoriginal, or just plain dull. On the whole, America has been proud of its unorthodoxy, and Americans often have made a new orthodoxy of being unorthodox. I hope that we can leave behind all emotional content of the word in what follows. By orthodox Christianity, I mean something purely descriptive. Orthodox Christianity is that form of Christianity which won the support of the overwhelming majority of Christians and which is expressed by most of the official proclamations or creeds of Christian groups.

At this point someone might object that it would be better to speak of orthodoxies instead of orthodoxy. Does not each of the multiple divisions of Christendom have its own orthodoxy? Each does, but there has been a central core of Christian doctrine that has held the allegiance of most Christians despite their differences. We are interested in that body of agreement.

Our search for orthodoxy must begin with the New Testament. The first Christians did not have any orthodoxy in the sense of a neatly formulated system of thought. Modern critical scholarship of the Bible has found that there are many theologies within the New Testament, but it has also found that beneath these variations in theology there is a common faith. The various theologies are the attempts of earnest men to think out and to express to others this common faith. Much of this faith is implicit rather than explicit. Twenty centuries have not been enough to work out all of the implications that lie in the basic faith of the New Testament.

The New Testament faith is based squarely upon the belief that in the life, death, and resurrection of the man Jesus, God entered into the life of man in a decisive fashion. That is why four accounts of the life of Jesus were passed down to us. That is why Christians faced the threat of dungeon, fire, and sword to spread their "Good News," which is what the word "Gospel" means. It is a distortion of history to suppose that Christianity began because a few men were persuaded by the brilliant ethical teaching of Jesus. On the contrary, the early Christians went out to tell the world of one whom God had proclaimed to be Lord.

We cannot overemphasize the importance of the Resurrection for the early Christians. Paul says, "If Christ be not raised, your faith is vain" (I Cor. 15:17). If you read this passage, you will see that he is not trying to persuade his fellow Christians that Christ arose; rather he is referring to the one point where there can be no difference between himself and his readers in order that he may go on to prove another point. The Resurrection was the one thing the early Christian could not deny and still consider himself a Christian. It was the rock of his faith.

Today the Resurrection often means to Christians nothing more than proof of life after death. It meant that to the early Christians, but it meant much more. Primarily, the Resurrection was the proof that Jesus was the Christ or Messiah of God. For centuries the Jews had lived on the promise that God was going to send his Messiah, his chosen agent, to save his people and to establish a society of justice. Quite naturally, since the Jews lived for centuries under foreign conquerors, they came to hope that the Messiah would be a military leader who would call upon the legions of heaven to overthrow the cruel oppressors. Finally, when Jesus came his followers dared to hope that he was the long-awaited Messiah. But he did not act as many had hoped the Messiah would act: he did not gather an army; he refused to be made a king. Finally, he was captured and spit upon and led out like a common criminal to be executed. He died beautifully, but the disciples wanted more than a beautiful death. A Messiah who had died, who was defeated and overcome by Rome, was hardly one who could save man. The disciples fled, not because they lacked courage but because there seemed no sense in risking one's life in a lost cause. They had made a tragic mistake and they felt they might as well admit it. But at the very depth of despair they were suddenly faced with a new development. Jesus was not dead: he was alive; he had risen.

What the Resurrection meant, therefore, was that

Jesus was after all the Messiah or agent of God. God had been working through him as the disciples had believed. Rome with its naked power was not the most powerful force in the world; Rome had set in motion a train of events that would eventually overcome it when it crucified the lowly Galilean carpenter. The forces of evil—and the early Christians believed that these included the demons as well as evil men—had risen to their greatest power and had done their worst. But, in the very moment of their victory, God had proved himself more powerful than they. Jesus had not achieved what they had hoped he would achieve, but as the days passed they realized that he had achieved something better. He had not freed them from Rome, but he had freed them from the chains that bound them to sin and death, chains that had held them in fear. He had revealed decisively that the power of good is greater than the power of evil.

In the Resurrection God had proved the superiority of the spirit of Jesus over the spirit of evil. Therefore the Christians looked forward to the return or Second Coming of Christ, when evil would be completely destroyed. The forces of evil had been defeated in the crucial battle; there could be no further doubt about the ultimate victor. But the evil forces were still in the field and still able to cause discomfort. The decisive battle had been won but the final battle was still to come.

The disciples went out into the pagan world with the message that God had spoken, God had acted, God had revealed his nature to man. Man need no longer climb the treacherous mountain path that leads to knowledge of God; God had come down from the mountain to allow men to see him. "God," they proclaimed, "was in Christ, reconciling the world unto himself" (II Cor. 5:19).

Though this faith was simple, it was full of implications. It meant that God was like Jesus; the spirit of Jesus revealed the nature of God. In a world where many voices were raised claiming to know all about God, the Christians dared to believe that God himself had broken through the clouds which hid his face. The one word that described the life and teaching of Jesus was "love." If God was like Jesus, then "God is love" (I John 4:8).

As time passed, the early term "Messiah," or "Christ," as it was translated into Greek, no longer seemed adequate to express this faith. This was particularly true as Christians went out to the Greek and Roman world where people had never heard of the Jewish Messiah. And so they began to call Jesus the "Lord," "Savior," "only begotten Son." All of these were terms by which Christians tried to express their belief that in Jesus God had made a unique revelation of himself to man. Finally, they came to say with Doubting Thomas, "My Lord and my God." Jesus had not been simply sent by God; he was God, God at work in the life of man.

Paul, the leading interpreter of Christianity during the New Testament period, led Christianity in its earliest battle—that against legalism. Every religion, including the Christian, tends to become legalistic. That is, it teaches that man must obey certain rules and regulations to win the favor and rewards of God.

Both Jesus and Paul fought against legalism. Jesus asserted that when a man had done everything that he could, he still was to count himself an unprofitable servant (Luke 17:10). That is, he was not to suppose that he had earned some kind of payment from God. Similarly, Jesus taught that God makes his rain to fall on the just and on the unjust (Matt. 5:45). God does not place an umbrella over the heads of those who are good so that they have a special protection from the slings and arrows of outrageous fortune. The slowness with which Christians have come to accept this basic fact in Jesus' teaching is strange. It still seems natural for many to suppose that a life of superior goodness will receive a superior reward, if not here, then surely hereafter. Jesus, however, explicitly denies this in his parable of the Laborers in the Vineyard (Matt. 20:1-16). The men who have worked from the dew of early morn and through the noontide heat do not receive any more pay at the end of the day than the men who worked but an hour.

The early Christians, led by Paul, came to see that legalism, the attempt to earn rewards from God by obeying certain rules, is basically wrong. It is wrong because it commercializes religion. One is good because he expects to get paid for his good deeds. It is wrong because it leads so easily to pride and hypocrisy, as we see in the Pharisees. Because the Pharisee keeps the law a little better than others, he feels far superior. Furthermore, he is continually tempted into the hypocrisy of believing that he is doing better than he really is. On the other hand, men like Paul found that legalism led to despair. As they realized how far short they were falling of the ideal goodness, they despaired of themselves, their salvation, and their reward.

In place of legalism, Jesus and Paul put the doctrine of salvation by grace through faith. The doctrine is implicit in Jesus and explicit in Paul. It is rooted in Jesus' assertion that God is a father. Every child who has loving parents knows the meaning of salvation by grace. The child does not earn his way into his parents' favor; he is loved simply because he exists. Before the child knows the meaning of love, he is surrounded with the tangible proofs of his parents' love. The true parent does not shower greater gifts upon the good son than upon the less good. True family life is not built upon a commercial basis of so much love for so much work; it is built freely upon grace, unearned love. The child is motivated, not by the desire to win greater favors from his parents, but by gratitude for the favors he has already received.

When the child from such a home "goes wrong," when he disappoints the hopes of his parents, he does not have to earn his way back into their favor. The parable of the Prodigal Son is a beautiful presentation of salvation by grace. After the son had disgraced his home and besmirched his own and his family's good name by riotous living with harlots, he found himself hobnobbing with the pigs. As he eked out his living with husks, he decided upon a scheme to earn his way back into his father's good graces. He would become a servant in his father's home. He had a nice little speech prepared, in which he was to offer himself as a servant to his father. But his father never gave him a chance to speak it. While the son was yet far off, the father ran to him and accepted him as a son, not as a servant.

We must be careful not to interpret this too sentimentally. It is not simply a matter of letting bygones be bygones. The true parent does not simply condone the erring boy. Robert Louis Stevenson, in *The Master of Ballantrae*, has told the story of a father who did simply condone his son's sin. Stevenson says of the father that forgiveness—to misuse a noble word—flowed from him like the weak tears of senility. True parental forgiveness is not like the tears of senility; it is rather like the Cross on Golgotha; it hurts the parent; it rends his soul. It is not easy to embrace the neck that was last caressed by harlots; it is not easy to forget the scorn and ridicule of the neighbors; but, despite the cost, the father forgives.

It is this family relationship which Jesus and Paul use to illustrate the free grace of God. God's love is not something that man has to purchase or deserve. "While we were yet sinners," says Paul, "Christ died for us" (Rom. 5:8). That is, before man had made himself good enough, God acted to save him. Through Jesus, God offers to man the promise that if he will but turn to God he will be received. This forgiveness is not an easy matter for God. Although Paul does not have any clear doctrine of the meaning of the Cross, he is certain that it represents the price that God had to pay to win man from sin. This forgiveness of God could be received by any man who would accept it in faith.

Faith does not mean, for Paul, believing something, although of course some belief must be involved in it. Faith is rather a giving of oneself. The Prodigal Son had faith when he arose to go home. Faith is, for Paul, a commitment which causes one to act in a certain fashion. Faith in God did not mean believing that there was a God or believing some doctrine about Jesus; it meant giving oneself over to being a son of God, to having that mind in oneself which was in Christ Jesus (Phil. 2:5).

It would be a mistake, however, to suppose that grace was simply God's willingness to forgive the man who came to him with faith. Grace also included the power of God which comes to a man and enables him to do those things that he could not do before. Jesus asserts that faith can move mountains, and Paul concedes that through faith he has found the power that he lacked to do those things which he had known that he ought to do but which he had not done. Paul teaches that we can live "in Christ" a new life of strength and power.

The grace of God frees a man from fear and the sense of guilt. He knows that he is accepted, even as he is, by God. He knows that neither life nor death nor principalities nor powers can remove him from the love of God that is in Christ Jesus (Rom. 8:38-39). But it also frees him from the bonds of habit, indolence, and weakness that tie him to sin. Down through Christian history men have affirmed that in Christ they found two great freedoms: the freedom from fear and the freedom from sin.

This was the simple core of Christian faith upon which Christian orthodoxy was built. Orthodoxy grew from the life that was lived in the light of this basic faith. Christian theology is not a philosophical system that was thought up by men in the quiet of an academic study. It was hammered out by men who were on the firing line of the Church. Every plank in the platform of orthodoxy was laid because some heresy had arisen which threatened to change the nature of Christianity and to destroy its central faith. In facing heresy, Christians were forced to think out the implications of their convictions. Because the doctrines of Christianity grew out of life and not out of classroom discussion, they cannot be understood by the man who, figuratively speaking, puts his feet on the mantelpiece and reads about them. They can only be understood by the man who shares the Christian life, who is ready to stand, as the writers of the doctrines stood, in the front lines of Christian living.

Like "orthodoxy," "heresy" is an emotionally charged term. We mean by it a misinterpretation of the orthodox position. The first great heresy, Gnosticism, arose in the second and third centuries. It was a movement that threatened Christianity from within at a time when the Roman emperors were threatening it from without, and of the two threats the Gnostics were the more dangerous. Rome could not kill Christianity, but Gnosticism, if it had been successful, would have perverted it.

The Gnostics were philosophers who wished to amalgamate all the world's religions by taking the best in each of them. In due time, many Gnostics found their way into the Church. They began to link up their ideas with Christianity, but in doing so they changed Christianity to fit their ideas.

The basic belief of the Gnostics was what we call dualism. That is, they believed that the world is ultimately divided between two powers, good and evil. In line with much Greek philosophy, they identified evil with matter. Because of this they rejected the God of the Old Testament who had created the world. The Creator of this evil world must be evil, they insisted.

Because the Gnostics identified evil with the material world, they sought salvation from it. All material things were evil and hindered the salvation of the soul. They believed that the soul could save itself by an ascetic denial of the flesh and by knowledge. In fact, the name Gnostic comes from the Greek word *gnosis*, which means knowledge. They were particularly concerned with the mystical forms of knowledge. Knowledge was to be kept secret and revealed only to the elite few who were initiated into the mysteries and who were worthy of learning the truth.

The Gnostics liked many things about Christianity. They liked the concept of Christ being sent by God. They taught that the good God had sent one of his subordinates, Christ, into the world to free the souls of men from the chains of matter into which they had been locked by the evil God of the Old Testament. Christ, however, could not allow his purity to be tainted by matter. He could not have been truly a man. It was not right that Christ should have been born of woman because, even if the woman was a virgin, they felt he could not have escaped contamination. It was equally unthinkable that the divine Christ should have eaten and drunk, have grown weary, and suffered and died. Different Gnostics used different arguments to get out of this dilemma. One group insisted that the divine Christ had adopted the human Jesus for a short time and had acted and spoken through him, but had fled from Jesus before the crucifixion. Another group insisted that Jesus did not really have a body at all; it was a clever hallucination. Whichever school a Gnostic belonged to, he agreed in denying that Jesus was in any sense a true human being. This Christian heresy did not deny that Jesus was divine; it denied that Jesus was human.

The Gnostics were very difficult to combat, for most of them lived pure lives. In a day when ascetism was widely extolled, their rigorous denial of the flesh won them considerable favor. In arguments they would always insist that they had some secret information that had been denied their opponent: Jesus had passed on this information to the elite Gnostics of his time and had hidden it from the materially blinded Jews who founded the Church. If this failed, Gnostics would claim a special revelation from heaven which proved their point. Yet Christianity had to cast out Gnosticism. If the Gnostics had triumphed, the message of Christianity to all men would have been replaced by a message for the chosen few. Its Christ would have ceased to be a human being and would have become like one of the many gods of the mystery religions—a vague and legendary figure. Christians would have been forced to abandon their priceless heritage from Judaism and become a world-denying ascetic band.

Christianity rose up to cast out this heresy, and in doing so it solidified its own orthodox position. The Apostles' Creed, which is still repeated in many churches, arose at this time, and can best be understood as a refutation of Gnosticism. First, it affirmed belief in "God, the Father Almighty, Maker of heaven and earth." That is, it repudiated the idea that the created world is evil or the work of an evil god. This material world is good and worthy to be used and enjoyed by man.

The Apostles' Creed next affirms belief in "Jesus Christ His only Son our Lord: who was conceived by the Holy Ghost, born of the Virgin Mary, suffered under Pontius Pilate, was crucified, dead and buried." Many a modern man has been stopped by the phrase "born of the Virgin Mary." He cannot believe in the Virgin Birth. But, ironically, to the early Gnostics, the problem was not "Virgin"; it was "born." The modern man sees a red flag because he hears "born of the *Virgin* Mary"; the Gnostic saw a red flag because he heard "*born* of the Virgin Mary." Actually, this phrase, together with the ones about suffering, death, and burial, was the Church's method of asserting its belief in the complete humanity of Jesus. Whatever orthodox Christianity had to say about the divinity of Jesus, it retained a firm hold on its belief in his humanity.

In the same light must be understood that other phrase of the Creed that causes trouble to many moderns—"The Resurrection of the body." Are we to believe, they ask, that the atoms of this earthly body will be regathered and made to live again? Actually, anyone who has read the fifteenth chapter of First Corinthians could not suppose that this is what the doctrine means. But it was a method of asserting the Jewish faith that man is a whole; he is not divided, as the Gnostics and many other Greek philosophers believed, into a good soul and an evil body. The Gnostic doctrine of the immortality of the soul is based on this belief, and implies that the soul is naturally immortal and only needs to be freed from the flesh. This also implies that the body is at best a burden and at worst an obstacle to the salvation of the soul. Christianity denied this, asserting the value of the body and thereby the importance of this earthly life.

The next great issue that came to the center of Christian thinking was that of the Trinity—the relationship of Father, Son, and Holy Spirit. This too was raised by the problem of heresy. Christians never sat down to think out the doctrine of the Trinity as a philosophical problem. Augustine summed it up when he said that the pronouncements upon the subject were not made to say something but in order that Christians might not be silent. That is, concepts had arisen which made silence impossible.

After considerable reflection, I have decided that it is impossible for me to make this doctrine clear to the reader in the space that I can devote to it. The best minds in Christendom debated for centuries before they came to any conclusion, and that debate, presupposing a full knowledge of the philosophies of the time, cannot be explained briefly. I shall limit myself to a few observations that will be helpful for our purpose.

The problem was debated at the Council of Nicaea in 325, from which we get the Nicene Creed found in the hymnbooks or Prayer Books of many modern denominations. Most people have heard the gibe that the Council of Nicaea saw a battle that nearly split Christendom apart and that the battle was over nothing but one "iota," the smallest letter in the Greek alphabet. It is true that the two sides at Nicaea were fighting over which of two words should be put into the creed and that the only difference in the spelling of the words was one Greek letter. One side wanted the word *homoousios* to say that Christ was of the same substance as God, and the other side wanted the word *homoiousios* to say that Christ was of a substance like to that of God. But only ignorance can go from that fact to the conclusion that the issues must have been unimportant.

I recall a story which appeared in a popular magazine a few years ago. It explained why telegraph and cable companies spell out punctuation marks instead of having just one signal for each of them. At one time, according to the story, there was a code signal for each punctuation mark. A woman, touring in Europe, cabled her husband as follows: "Have found wonderful bracelet. Price seventy-five thousand dollars. May I buy it?" The husband promptly cabled back, "No, price too high." The cable operator, in transmitting the message, missed the signal for the comma. The woman received a message which read,

"No price too high." She bought the bracelet; the husband sued the company and won. Ever since, the users of Morse code have spelled out punctuation. This anecdote serves to remind us that the importance of a message cannot be weighed by the size of the punctuation or the number of letters involved. Although only an iota divided the parties at Nicaea, the issues involved represented two completely different interpretations of the Christian faith.

The problem of the Trinity arises from the Christian belief that God was acting in and through Jesus Christ. In the fourth century Arius put forward the theory that Christ was a lesser god created by God. This lesser god came to earth in the man Jesus who was not really a man at all, but a divine being freed from the normal limitations of humanity. If the Arian party could have got their iota into the creed, their point of view would have become orthodox Christianity. It would have meant that Christianity had degenerated to the polytheistic stage of paganism. It would have had two gods and a Jesus who was neither God nor man. It would have meant that God himself was unapproachable and apart from man. The result would have been to make of Christianity another pagan mystery religion.

The Nicene Creed asserted that God and Christ were of the same substance. This was the attempt to say in the philosophy of the time that there is only one God. He is active in creating and sustaining the world (as the Father); he was in Jesus Christ (as the Son); and he moves in the heart of the believer (as the Holy Spirit). The Nicene Creed rejected any attempt to think of three gods bound into some kind of unity. Christians have often come to think of Father, Son, and Holy Spirit as three gods, but when they have done so, they have erred from the path of orthodoxy. The criticism, made by Mohammedans, Jews, and Unitarians, that orthodox Christianity has three gods and that it has lost the monotheism of the Old Testament is based upon misunderstanding.

One of the complicating factors is that Trinitarian doctrine speaks of "Three Persons" but one God. The word "person" did not mean to the early thinkers what it means today. To us, a person means someone like Tom, Dick, or Harry. But the Latin word *persona* originally meant a mask which was worn by an actor on the stage. In Trinitarian thought the "mask" is not worn by God to hide but to reveal his true character. It is clear that when we think of the Trinity, we should not try to think of three persons in our sense of the term. Augustine's interpretation became orthodox, if not universal, for the West. He believed that if man is created in the image of God, he is created in the image of the Trinity. Hence he used analogies from the human mind to explain the Trinity. The Trinity is like the memory, intelligence, and will in the mind of a man. In short, as Augustine interprets the Trinity, we do not have to think of three persons when we think of God; but we may think of one person. Of course, Augustine made it clear that this was only an analogy; he was far too profound a thinker to suppose that God was a glorified man sitting in heaven. But if we are to speak at all about the mystery that is God, we must speak in analogies, and the analogy for the Trinity is not three men but one.

The Trinity was important, not simply because it

saved Christianity from the return to paganism but because it also gave the Christian assurance that it was God who was in, and responsible for, Jesus Christ. Man's salvation did not hang from the slender thread of what man himself had achieved, nor did it depend upon what some divine being less than God had done. Man could have the courage to overcome fear and doubt because God himself had acted for him and had revealed himself as a God of love and mercy.

The Trinitarian controversy was followed by what we know as the Christological controversy. This controversy was fought out in the Council of Chalcedon in 451 and issued in the Creed of Chalcedon. In a sense, it may be said that the Trinitarian controversy was over the nature of God in heaven. What is God like, if Jesus was divine? The Christological doctrine tried to see what Jesus, on earth, was like if he were divine. Nicaea had decided that there was but one God and that Jesus was fully divine, the act of the one God. But immediately men began to wonder how Jesus could be both divine and human. How could the eternal, unchanging perfect God take on the limitations of a man? Many people felt that he could not.

One group of thinkers, known as Apollinarians, arose who, in effect, admitted that Jesus had a human body (they could not deny that without falling into the old Gnostic error), but they denied that he had a true human personality. The Second Person of the Trinity took the place of a human personality in Jesus' body. Despite the fact that Jesus was allowed a body, this did not make him any more human than the Gnostics had done. It was still impossible to believe with the Bible that he "was in all points tempted like as we are" (Heb. 4:15). The other side argued that there were two natures in Jesus, a human spirit and the spirit of God. These two became fused by the fact that the human Jesus gave himself over completely to the divine so that there was a moral unity. This view, known as Nestorianism, gave Jesus moral freedom and the possibility of temptation, but it seemed to leave Jesus with a dual or even with a split personality.

The decision at Chalcedon is altogether too complex to analyze in our space, and authorities still debate its implications. But this fact can be seen: the orthodox faith was settled as the belief that Jesus was truly divine, the work of God, and that he was truly and completely human. Chalcedon repudiated any theory that would deny either the humanity or the divinity of Jesus. There is no doubt that this was the faith of the earliest Christians, and as such Chalcedon was true to that faith. But it is also clear that the problem of how Christ could be both human and divine remains unsolved. We shall see that the question arises again in modern theology.

It is easy to be critical of those early Church conferences at Nicaea and Chalcedon. There were many instances of petty personal jealousies, national clashes, political maneuvering, and power politics. And yet, as one looks back over the perspective of history, it is hard to doubt that some divine guidance was also at work. Despite the mortal weaknesses that were so evident, the Church set its face squarely against the forces which would have robbed Christianity of its monotheism and its historical Jesus and which would have pulled Christianity down to the level of pagan faiths. It is well to keep this in mind as we grow impatient with very similar mortal weaknesses that are evident in the present World Council of Churches as it tries to think through the implications of faith for today. It is easy for us to see its weakness, but future historians may also see the hand of God in the work of the Council.

The great father of orthodoxy for Western thought was Augustine. He is a Catholic saint, and yet the Protestant Reformation leaned more heavily upon him than upon any other pre-Reformation thinker. We have already mentioned his contribution to the doctrine of the Trinity. Augustine was one of those rare mental geniuses who occur once in a thousand years. Modern thought owes him many an unacknowledged debt. Augustine drove men's thoughts inward to self-analysis, and, as one modern writer has pointed out, about the only thing Augustine could learn from modern psychology would be its jargon. Unfortunately, we can mention only one aspect of this great thinker's contribution: it was he who brought most forcefully into orthodox thought the concept of Original Sin.

Before Augustine, Christian thought had expressed its faith that Jesus, as the revelation of God, was also the revelation of what man was created to be. But, if this is the case, something seems to have gone wrong. Man, with his pettiness, his vindictiveness, his ceaseless crimes, both those of commission and of omission, is far from having in him the spirit that was in Jesus. To this, orthodoxy had said that man had fallen. Adam, the first man, had used his God-given freedom of choice to choose against God and had pulled mankind down with him. Christ was sent to restore man to his original position.

Augustine's doctrine, like the rest of orthodoxy, was worked out against a heresy. The heresy was that of an English monk, Pelagius. Pelagius insisted that every man is completely free to choose either good or evil at every moment in his life. He insisted that Adam's fall had affected no one but Adam. Against this Augustine denied that man is free in this sense to do either good or evil. Working with what reminds us of modern depth psychology, Augustine insisted that the pull of the race is stronger than Pelagius realized. The individual cannot start with a clean slate; he bears his society, his heritage, with him. Because that heritage is sinful, man is prone to sin; he has a bias toward sin so great that, but for the helping grace of God, he cannot overcome it. Instead of being free, man is actually bound to his way of sin and only becomes truly free as God gives him the grace to break through his bonds.

Augustine located the source of original sin, that is, the inherited weakness or inability to do good, in man's pride. Turning to the story of Adam, Augustine pointed out that Adam was free; he had everything he could desire in the Garden of Eden. But Adam desired one more thing: he desired to be free from God; he resented his dependence upon God; he wished to take the place of God. So, at the lure of the serpent that he might become as God, he ate the fruit of the tree. That is, man's refusal to accept his position as a creature, to be what he was made, leads him to seek to be equal with God, his creator. When man refuses to give God the proper place in life, the result is concupiscence, the unrestrained lust after the things of this world. Because God ceases to be the center of life, man falls into the other sins: greed, lust, robbery, murder, selfishness. The word "concupiscence," however, had also the implications of sex. At first, with Augustine, sex was only one of the many lusts for the things of the world which plague man; but there was a tendency both in Augustine and in his followers to emphasize sex above the other sins.

Adam's sin was passed down to his descendants. Because each descendant is procreated through sex, there is a twofold source of sin. The sexual origin of each man is sinful, and the tendency to sin is also inherited as a congenital weakness.

If we are to understand the modern theologians who return to this doctrine, we must see that in Augustine there are actually two distinct elements. First, there is a psychological analysis of man. According to this, pride, which is a basic weakness of man, explains the great gulf between what man was created to be and what he is. Here the source of man's ills is a spiritual one. But, in explaining how this began and how it is transmitted, you have Augustine's doctrine about Adam and the inheritance of his sinful traits. It would almost seem that the spiritual nature of sin has been turned into a biological taint. It is not easy to reconcile the spiritual analysis of sin with the biological transmission of it. Certainly, it is possible, as we shall see, to agree with Augustine's spiritual analysis while rejecting his theory of inheritance.

Augustine's theory led him to the doctrine of predestination. This never became orthodox for all Christians, but we meet it again in Calvinistic orthodoxy. If man cannot save himself, if God's grace must save him, how does God decide whom he will aid? It cannot be, felt Augustine, that God foresees someone earning grace, for it is a free gift. If you read Augustine's *Confessions*, the autobiography of his spiritual life, you will find him expressing again and again his wonder that God had saved *him*. He was certain that he had done nothing to deserve it. It was no credit to him that he no longer walked the paths of error and sin in which once he had delighted. God had acted upon him in a way that could not have been foreseen. God had chosen or elected him for salvation.

When the Reformation occurred, the Reformers did not, for the most part, question any of these doctrines of orthodoxy that we have been tracing. Luther returned to the doctrine of salvation by grace, emphasizing it in a way in which it had not been emphasized since Paul. This brought him into sharp conflict with the Catholic doctrines about the nature of the Church and authority within it. Renouncing the pope's claim to supremacy, Luther found the ultimate authority in the Bible as it was interpreted by the Holy Spirit working within a man's heart. In the place of the Catholic hierarchy he placed the doctrine of the priesthood of all believers. That is, no man needed a priest to mediate between him and God except Christ,

who is the perfect mediator, the perfect priest for all
men.

Calvin followed Luther and gave us the first systematic Protestant theology. The center of theology
for Calvin was God and his chief aim was to glorify
God. Any kind of faith in the natural ability or
power of man was, to Calvin, faith in a bruised and
broken reed. But where man was helpless God was
almighty. God could be trusted to do what man could
not. Thus Calvin followed Augustine's doctrine of
predestination.

The doctrine of predestination is difficult for
modern man to understand. Yet, ironically, modern
man is quite ready to accept theories of determinism which deny any freedom or dignity to man.
These modern doctrines are more hopeless than those
of Calvin, for there is no God of mercy in them to
modify the iron necessity of determinism. Predestination was important for the Calvinist as a basis for
assurance. The Roman Catholic was certain of his salvation because he was in the one true Church. The
Protestants took the courageous step of repudiating
such certainty and risked their salvation itself in order
that they might follow their consciences. The doctrine
of predestination was the Calvinist answer to Catholic
certainty. The salvation of man does not depend, said
Calvin, upon membership in an institution. Salvation
is a matter between a man and his God. We must
trust God to save his elect. The differences that divide
one group of men from another are of no importance
to God.

There is one last plank in the platform of orthodoxy that must be mentioned, the doctrine of atonement. Every religion has had to deal with the concept of atonement. If you believe that God has any requirements which man fails to fulfill, then you are faced with the problem of how God can be reconciled. If you have injured a friend or neighbor, you have the problem of atonement, the problem of reestablishing the fellowship that has been broken.

In contrast to other religions, Christianity has a unique point of view. Whereas most religions believe that man has to do something to atone to God, Christianity teaches that God himself has performed the atoning work. Other religions perform sacrifices in order that God might turn his angry face back toward man and forgive him. Christianity teaches that God has performed a sacrifice, in and through Jesus, which has brought God and man back into fellowship with each other. But the problem arises: What did God do? Paul is clear that Jesus' death was central, but he gives no clear explanation. The Church never held a council on this doctrine, as it did on the Trinity and the nature of Christ. No one doctrine has been held from the beginning, and hence it is difficult to speak of the orthodox position.

The so-called classical doctrine of atonement was accepted for more than a thousand years. According to this, Satan had gained the souls of men because they had sinned. But God made a bargain with Satan: he would give Satan the soul of Jesus, even though Satan did not deserve him, if Satan would release the souls of men who accepted Jesus. Satan agreed, thinking that Jesus was only a good man. But when he received Jesus, he found that he could not hold him for he was the Son of God. And so Satan ended up with neither the souls of those who accepted Christ nor Christ himself. This doctrine sounds crude and seems to implicate God in a rather shady trick upon the Devil. It has, none the less, two profound thoughts. It expresses faith that in the death and resurrection of Jesus, God has conquered the forces of evil. Good is more powerful than evil. In the second place, it points to the fact that evil tends to overreach and thus destroy itself. "Give a man enough rope and he will hang himself." This is a fact of life. If Hitler, for example, had been content with a little less he might still rule Germany. Evil cannot be satisfied, and in its insatiable greed it brings destruction upon itself. But despite these insights, the doctrine seemed too crude, and in the eleventh century two new doctrines were put forward.

The first came from Anselm. He argued that man owed obedience to God, the ruler of the universe, but he had failed to obey and hence he fell into debt to God. He had dishonored God. Justice demanded either that the debt be paid to God or that man be punished. Either way would uphold God's prestige as the moral ruler of man. But God did not want to punish man eternally, for his purpose in creating man was to have fellowship with him. Man could not give God satisfaction since man already owed perfect obedience and could do no more. If God waved the sin aside and simply forgave, his honor and prestige as the ruler would be called into question. We have a dilemma; man owed the debt, but only God could pay it. So, God sent Jesus, who was both God and man. Because he was God, he could pay the debt; because he was also man he could pay it for man. But even Jesus could not pay it by living a perfect life, for, as man, he already owed that to God. But Jesus did not deserve to die since he had not sinned. Consequently, when Jesus gave himself over to death, he paid the debt for man. God's honor was vindicated so that he could forgive those who came to him through Christ.

This theory did not express perfectly what the Church wanted to say and it was never accepted officially. It made God sound very much like a feudal lord who was afraid his serfs might get out of hand if he appeared too lenient. Yet it did express the Church's belief that forgiveness is not something simple or easy. It costs God to forgive.

Abélard presented another theory. He insisted that there was nothing on God's side that made forgiveness impossible. But forgiveness is a two-way affair. You cannot forgive a man who does not wish to be forgiven. Forgiveness means the restoration of broken fellowship; but one cannot restore the fellowship if the other does not wish it restored. This, says Abélard, was God's problem. He wanted to forgive man, but man went his merry way sinning and did not repent or ask forgiveness. So God acted; he sent his Son to suffer and die for man as a manifestation of God's great love. When man sees this he is moved to shame and repents so that God is able to forgive him.

Abélard's doctrine also says something that orthodox Christianity wanted to say. In the death of Christ we see the love of God in such a way that we are moved to repent. None the less, Abélard's doctrine won him the charge of heresy. The orthodox argument against it usually goes like this: If a man jumps into the water and saves me while I am drowning, the act reveals his love. But if we are walking along the beach and he suddenly says, "See how much I love you," and then jumps into the water and drowns, we are inclined to think the sun got too hot for him. In other words, Christ's death can only be a revelation of God's love for man if it was a necessary sacrifice. It is meaningless if man could be saved without it.

Orthodox Christianity, while it was not completely satisfied with Anselm, usually has taken some form of his theory. Christ, it has believed, was in some sense our substitute; he died to pay our debt or he suffered the punishment that we ought to have suffered for our sin. Protestant orthodoxy was inclined to put the doctrine in terms of the law courts. Man had committed crimes for which he must be punished, but Jesus "took the rap" in man's place. So interpreted, the doctrine has the effect of Abélard's; it wins man to repent, but it does so because the sacrifice was a necessary one and not a grand gesture.

This is the main outline of the orthodox position in theology upon which Christians from widely separated denominations would agree. It is this body of thought, with a few implications that we shall see as we go along, that we have in mind when we speak of orthodox Christianity.

2

The Threat to Orthodoxy

In the last chapter we spoke of the rise of orthodoxy. Even there it was evident that not all Christians were orthodox, for orthodoxy was normally clarified only when someone put forth a heresy. In this chapter we will concentrate upon the unorthodox. If we were attempting a complete history of unorthodoxy, we should begin here with the early Christians as we did in the last chapter. But our purpose is not that; we desire only to interpret the modern field and so will limit ourselves to what is helpful for that purpose. Since our concern is with Protestant thought, we will limit ourselves to the period since the Reformation.

As man entered the modern world, there was a two-fold threat to orthodoxy. One threat came from outside the Church and spoke through secular philosophies. The other threat came from within the Church itself, where an increasing number of Christians became dissatisfied with orthodoxy. There is a relation between these two movements but there is also a distinction. We shall first look at the secular thought and later return to developments within Christianity itself. Since the secular developments are better known than the religious, we shall deal more fully with the latter.

At the time of the Reformation there was another powerful current of thought, already two hundred years old: the Renaissance. It began by looking back and rediscovering the ancient Greek and Roman culture in which was to be found a spirit of life quite different from that of medieval Europe. Some of the Renaissance thinkers were indifferent or antagonistic to religion; some were friendly to religion; and some, like Melanchthon and Zwingli, were leaders of the Reformation. But there was a tendency in most of the Renaissance thinkers to leave orthodoxy. Erasmus, for example, tried to be a loyal son of the Roman Catholic Church, but his writings won the condemnation of his Church's authorities. The Renaissance was characterized by faith in man and interest in this world. Compared to the medieval preoccupation with life after death, the Renaissance was relatively uninterested in the subject. Because of the Renaissance's faith in reason, it did not see any necessity for revelation from God. It was not interested in theology or in the sacramental aspects of the Church. Religion to the thinkers of this school was the cornerstone of ethics.

The Renaissance was deeply interested in restoring the thought of the ancient world and began to work out a science to restore the original wording of manuscripts. In due time, this interest led men to reconsider the manuscripts of the Bible, and here was one place where Erasmus won the displeasure of his Church. Luther, however, in translating the Bible, made use of these results of Renaissance scholarship.

The eighteenth century, the century of rationalism and enlightenment, brought the strongest secular blows against orthodoxy. The rationalists were men who believed in reason with a profound faith. They rebelled against all authorities outside man's reason and claimed for reason an autonomy which would enable it to examine all questions without interference. The rationalists were by no means irreligious men. John Locke, for example, believed that no tolerance could be shown to atheists, for they threatened the very structure of Western civilization upon which tolerance and our other ideals must rest. But if rationalism was not anti-religious, it was anti-orthodox. It wanted a religion, as Kant put it, within the bounds of reason only.

Among the attacks of rationalism upon orthodoxy was Hume's argument against the likelihood of miracles. Hume did not deny the possibility of miracles; his own philosophy would have made such a denial contradictory. But he did argue that miracles would always be less probable than some alternative explanation. Despite the fact that Hume's argument tended to be circular, he was widely hailed as having disproved miracles. It became next to impossible for orthodoxy to prove the truth of its faith by pointing to the miracle stories of the Bible.

Immanuel Kant attacked the so-called proofs of God. These were not necessarily central to orthodoxy, for the Church did not worry much about proving God until the thirteenth century, when Thomas Aquinas supplied his famous five proofs. Nevertheless, it shook orthodoxy to find that reason could not establish beyond doubt the existence of God. Kant himself argued that if pure reason could not find God, the practical demands of moral living could. But Kant's God was hardly the God of orthodoxy. For Kant only three religious postulates were necessary for the moral life: God, the freedom of man, and immortality.

Although Kant, in his last writings, returned to a concept of radical evil, the rationalists as a whole were opposed to any doctrine of original sin. They had great confidence that man's reason was good and could solve all of man's problems.

At the same time that rationalism was attacking orthodox religion, natural science was arising. Many foolish things have been written about the conflict of science and religion. Usually science is pictured as a knight in shining armor, always following the gleam of truth, while religion is the stupid dragon that tries to devour truth. This picture, which owes much to Andrew Dickson White's monumental work *A History of the Warfare of Science with Theology in Christendom,* is only partly true. In every conflict over science, there were many sincerely religious and orthodox men who fought for the acceptance of science. On the other hand, there were many men of science who fought against the new scientific developments. We need another book to balance the scales, one which might be called *A History of the Warfare of Science with Science.* Actually, what happened was that the whole cultural feeling of an age rose up in protest against new world views that would shatter the comfortable picture of the universe that was accepted. Religion, as a powerful and organized force in society, often became the center of the anti-scientific protest.

As a result, religion, particularly in its orthodox forms, became discredited. It seemed that science was always proved right and religion wrong. The idea began to arise that science could solve all of man's problems, that it was only ignorance and inertia, particularly the ignorance and inertia of the churches, which were holding back the forward march of science, the new savior.

There were two doctrines of science that particularly disturbed orthodox religion, those of Copernicus and Darwin. The medieval world pictured a universe in which the earth was the center and man the supreme form of life upon earth. Copernicus opened the door to a universe so vast that the earth shrank to a mere grain of sand, lost in space. It seemed ridiculous to many people to suppose that either the earth or man could be important to God, if there was a God. Darwin's theory of evolution broke down the barriers between man and the animal world. Man appeared as simply a highly developed animal. In place of the intelligent love of a Creator who gave each animal its shape and form, Darwin pictured a ruthless struggle for existence among life forms, with victory going to those best fitted to survive. Although at first the doctrine of evolution seemed to doom man to an unending battle for existence, it came in time to lay a foundation for the high hopes of progress that had grown in the rationalist movement. Herbert Spencer was particularly responsible for this. Man had evolved to his present high estate from the amoeba and he was destined, by a law of nature, to keep on progressing to perfection. The orthodox picture of the fall of man was made to look ridiculous. Man had not fallen; he had started out as a mere beast and, over a relatively short time, considering the age of the universe, had risen to unbelievable heights. Before him stretched an unending future of promise. This idea gripped both the intellectuals and the man in the street. The continual advance of invention led the average man to look condescendingly upon the ways of his fathers and to look forward to the even greater things that were to come. As Harry Emerson Fosdick said, man no longer desired to die and go to heaven; he wanted to live a hundred years to see what new wonders the inventive genius of man would bring forth.

As man began to look ahead with hope, he became increasingly dissatisfied with the imperfections of his social system. Karl Marx became a leading spokesman for the hope of a better earthly society. As he saw it, religion was one of the barriers to a better earthly life. Religion fed men upon hopes of heaven so that they did not revolt against those who were exploiting them in this life. Even among those who did not follow Marx, there was a widespread feeling that orthodox religion was an enemy of man's hope for a better and more decent life.

With the rise of modern psychology, Freud added new charges against religion. Not only was religion outmoded in its world view, the enemy of science and of progress, it was also, Freud claimed, wish fulfillment, a childish refusal to face the facts of life. By the end of the nineteenth century it had become increasingly impossible for the intellectuals to hold any religion and almost completely impossible for them to hold orthodox Christianity. Nietzsche spoke for a growing number when he proclaimed that "God is dead." Yet there were a few who trembled at the implications. For as Nietzsche saw so clearly, if God is dead, so are the moral traditions of the ages. Man is to replace God by remaking morality, and it is the supermen who must remake it.

If religion in general and orthodoxy in particular were having a difficult time in the secular world, orthodoxy was equally under attack within religion. We must now look at this.

The Reformation was not one movement but four, although the four were vitally related. In addition to the Lutheran and Calvinist movements, there was, in England, the Anglican movement. And, in both England and on the Continent, there were the so-called sectarian groups, including the Anabaptists, Baptists, Congregationalists, Quakers, Mennonites, and scores of smaller groups. The first three Reformation movements were orthodox in our sense of the term. So, for the most part, were the sectarians. But in this latter group there were actual and potential threats to orthodoxy.

The sects broke with the other Reformation groups over the doctrine of the Church. For them, the Church was to consist only of the saints, that is, practicing and fully convinced Christians. They deplored the taking of babies into the Church by infant baptism, for only those who lived the Christian life ought to be in the Church, they believed.

Because the sectarians emphasized that each Church member should be a practicing Christian, they were suspicious of the doctrine of salvation by grace. They saw too many people who used the doctrine as an excuse for not living Christian lives. Their protest gained more cogency as the years passed, and the second generation of Reformation leaders began to interpret salvation by faith to mean salvation by belief. Instead of faith being the commitment of one's life to God, as it had been for Paul and Luther, it meant believing the orthodox creeds and doctrines. In their reaction against the abuses of such a system, the sectarians were willing to run the risk of falling into a new legalism. The teachings of Jesus became rules that had to be followed by anyone who would join the Church.

Many of these groups, led by the Quaker George Fox, had a doctrine of the inner inspiration of each man by the Holy Spirit, or Inner Light. There was nothing unorthodox about this, as Christians have always believed that the Holy Spirit speaks to the heart of man and guides him. Both Luther and Calvin laid a great emphasis upon it. But there was a tendency in sectarian circles to find the ultimate authority in the Inner Light rather than in the Bible. In time this led to a radical criticism of the Bible and orthodoxy.

By the year 1600, a radical Protestantism had arisen to attack orthodoxy. It was known as Socinianism after its founder Fausto Socinus, who fled to Poland to escape persecution both by Catholics and by Protestants. This movement was the forerunner of modern Unitarianism and modern liberalism. The Socinians accepted the Bible but not uncritically. They found many errors in it. They insisted that nothing can be the revelation of God which is against reason and common sense or which is morally useless. On this basis many biblical stories were discredited.

The orthodox doctrine of the Trinity was rejected because of the inadequacy of the Greek philosophical concepts which had been used in the writing of the creeds. It was denied that Jesus had a divine nature, although it was granted that he was a higher type of man, a superman, so to speak.

The doctrine of original sin was discarded as irrational. Man still has the same freedom to choose between good and evil that Adam had. A hereditary sin is contradictory; there is no sin without guilt, and if we are guilty before we are born we must have sinned before we were born, which is ridiculous.

The idea that Jesus could have borne the punishment for our guilt is immoral and absurd, insisted the Socinians. One man cannot be punished justly in place of another. God needs no such scheme, for he is willing to forgive freely when man turns to him.

The Socinian faith was reduced to what was felt to be the bare essentials. Socinians believed that God rewarded and punished men, in an afterlife, for their obedience or disobedience to the ethical law taught most clearly by Jesus. The Resurrection and other Bible miracles were the proofs that Jesus spoke with divine authority.

With the rise of rationalism, a new religious movement, Deism, came to the fore. The Socinians had been concerned to be Christian, but the Deists looked for a religion that would be common to all rational men of good will. The Deists were repelled by the religious wars of the seventeenth century and the heresy hunting of the age. One of its first thinkers, Lord Herbert of Cherbury (died 1648), argued that a rational religion must be independent of any special revelation. The first tenet of such a religion is God, who can be proved to exist by the fact that the world needs a creator. Since there is a God, he deserves to be adored and obeyed, which means that man must live ethically. When we fail to do this, we must repent and strive to overcome our sins. Since this life does not bring adequate reward for goodness and punishment for evil, there must be another life in which the accounts are settled.

The God of the Deists has sometimes been called the watchmaker-God. God created the world as a watchmaker makes a watch, and then wound it up and let it run. Since God was a perfect "watchmaker," there was no need of his interfering with the world later. Hence the Deists rejected anything that seemed to be an interference of God with the world, such as miracles or a special revelation through the Bible.

The Deists believed that their religion was the original religion of man. From it had come, by distortion, all other religions. These distortions were the work of priests who concocted the theologies, myths, and doctrines of the various religions in order to enhance their own power.

Deism never got down to the common man; it was a religion for intellectuals only. Its power among the intellectuals is attested by the influence that it had upon the writing of the Declaration of Independence in America. The critique which Kant made of the proofs of God was a more serious blow to the Deists than it was to the orthodox, for rational proof of God was far more central to the former than to the latter.

As the modern world began to become smaller, Christians had to face the fact that theirs was not the only religion in the world. Of course, this was not discovered for the first time. For centuries Europe had trembled in fear of Mohammedan conquest. But the day came when the Christian began to meet individuals from other religions; he began to read their literature and to digest the meaning of their faith. A new science, Comparative Religions, grew up to study non-Christian religions. This movement was spurred by Deism, with its faith in the simple universal religion that had originally been held by all men. Ironically, research into other religions broke down this Deist theory instead of supporting it.

Several disturbing facts for orthodoxy came from this new science. Parallels to many Christian beliefs were found among non-Christian religions. Every religion abounded in miracle stories, and if Christianity was proved true by miracles, as even the Socinians thought, what of the miracles in other faiths? Every religion had its sacred Scriptures, claiming to be revealed. Why then suppose that the Christian Scriptures are superior? Furthermore, men who were primarily interested in the ethical consequences of religion found that other religions also had high ethical teaching. In short, the uniqueness of Christianity was questioned and challenged.

Another important nineteenth century develop-

ment was biblical criticism. The term "criticism" is
somewhat misleading. It is not meant to imply tearing
the Bible to pieces, although to many an orthodox
Christian that is what seemed to be happening. Actually, the Bible critic is simply a scholar who studies
the Bible to find its more exact meaning. He is critical in the sense that he tries to find rational or scientific reasons for his conclusions rather than to accept
the dogmas of the Church. Albert Schweitzer points
out that some of the first critics to contribute to our
knowledge of the New Testament were enemies of
Christ, men who looked at the Bible critically because they hoped to destroy the religion based upon
it. But the Church quickly took Bible criticism into
itself, and as time passed the seminaries became the
centers of critical research. This was not achieved without a battle, but the critics slowly won their case, although many a scholar lost his position in the process.

Biblical criticism came to be expressed in two forms,
the lower and higher criticism. The terms are purely
technical and do not imply any value judgments. The
lower critic dealt with problems of the text, and tried
to weigh the merits of the great many manuscripts of
the Bible which have been discovered in order that
he might find the earliest and most reliable text of
the Bible. The only aspects of lower criticism that
were new in the modern world were the greater ex-
actness with which ancient manuscripts could be
dated and read and the greater abundance of ancient manuscripts which have been discovered. Lower
critics did not produce anything which shook orthodoxy unduly.

Higher criticism begins where lower criticism leaves off. The higher critic is not primarily interested in the accuracy of the text; he is interested in the meaning of the words. He wishes to read between the lines and get behind the text to the events as they really happened. To do so, he must find out when each passage of Scripture was written, who wrote it, and to whom and why it was written. The higher critic believes that we can only understand the Bible if we can see it against this kind of background. For example, a Psalm takes on quite a different meaning when the critic concludes that it was not written by David, as tradition believed, but that it was a folk song that grew out of the sufferings of the Jews while they were in exile.

Higher criticism is no more a modern discovery than lower. From the second century to the present we find Christian writers using a higher critical approach to enable them to understand the Bible. But in the modern period a new weapon came into the hands of the critic—that of historical criticism. This new method had been developed by the later Renaissance and was improved by students of history. It was applied first to the books of the ancient world where it detected many forgeries and revised ideas of authorship in ancient manuscripts. In the nineteenth century this method was applied to the Bible as if the Bible were any other ancient book whose credentials had to pass the bar of historical method. This did result in many discoveries that shook orthodoxy.

Some of the results of higher criticism which

alarmed orthodoxy may be quickly mentioned. Critics generally agreed that Moses did not write the first five books of the Bible, as had been believed. Instead they were written by at least four different writers. Among other things, this meant that we have two different stories of Creation in Genesis. Critics believed that books and passages which purport to tell the future had been written after the events which presumably they had forecast. It came to be generally accepted that the Gospel of John, long the favorite Gospel of the orthodox, was not written by the Apostle John and that it is not good history. The first three Gospels, called the Synoptics, were dated much earlier than John's and were considered more reliable. More important, however, than any of these details was the fact that doubt was thrown upon the belief that the Bible is an infallible authority upon all things which it mentions.

One of the important developments of higher criticism was the search for the "historical Jesus." This term is interesting, for it implies that Jesus, as he lived in history, was different from the Jesus that we find portrayed in the Gospels. Critics tried to read between the lines and find out what Jesus had really been like. They assumed that the early Church and the Gospel writers had added many things to the biblical account so that the problem was to sift the authentic sayings and doings of Jesus from the later additions. Scores of lives of Jesus were written during the nineteenth century, each claiming that it portrayed the true Jesus. Two of the best known are *The Life of Jesus* by David Friedrich Strauss (1835–1836) and Renan's *The Life of Jesus* (1863). Although the various "lives" contradicted each other at many points, they did agree in removing the miraculous elements. They all assumed that science had proved miracles to be impossible, and they agreed that Jesus had not taught that he was the Messiah or that the world was coming to an end when he would return to set up the Kingdom of God. The *reductio ad absurdum* came when some of these critics decided that, since the Gospel records were so unreliable, there never was a Jesus at all. He was a myth invented by the early Church. This view was easily discredited, but it bothered many an orthodox thinker for a while.

Albert Schweitzer, in his book *The Quest of the Historical Jesus* (1906), has written a brilliant history of this epoch and reveals how most of the biographies of Jesus were simply the pictures of what the writers wanted to find. They did not describe Jesus, the Galilean carpenter of the first century, but a figure who taught and acted like a nineteenth century intellectual. Yet there was cold comfort for the orthodox in Schweitzer's book. Schweitzer found that Jesus did teach he was the Messiah and that he believed that the Kingdom of God was about to come down from heaven to remake the earth. The ethics which Jesus taught were simply the ethics for living during the short interval before he returned on the clouds of heaven to usher in a new day. Jesus went to his death in the rather pathetic illusion that by so doing he would hasten the coming of the Kingdom.

European Christianity met the challenge of these various developments by two schools of thought which, in turn, affected American thought. The first began with Friedrich Schleiermacher (1768–1834). He found that the prevailing rationalism of the eighteenth century had been replaced by the romanticism of the nineteenth. Where formerly cold reason had been the highest pursuit of man, now emotion and feeling moved into a prominent place. Against this background, Schleiermacher tried to rehabilitate religion among the intellectuals who had, for the most part, forsaken it during the eighteenth century.

Schleiermacher insisted that the great debates over proofs of God, the authority of Scriptures, miracles, and the like, were all on the outside fringe of religion. The heart of religion was and always had been feeling, not rational proofs and discussions. The God of religion is not, as much speculation seemed to imply, a theory dragged in to explain the universe. God, to the religious man, is an experience, a living reality. Religion is based on feeling or intuition. Schleiermacher analyzed this feeling in terms of dependence upon the universe. He pointed out that every man has to come to terms with the universe, the source of his being. All great art and literature has a concept of the totality of the universe, and this is, whether it is recognized or not, an experience of God. Unfortunately, this has been obscured by the traditional religionists. They have identified religion with creeds, and men who could no longer accept the creeds thought that they were through with religion. But this was a tragic mistake, for they still were in contact with God through their feeling of dependence upon the universe.

For Schleiermacher religion is essentially ethical because when one becomes aware of his dependence upon the universe he is immediately aware of his relationship with his fellow men, who are likewise bound to the source of their being. In all religions we find this primary experience of man, and it is expressed in various doctrines and forms. But if the forms become too important we must get rid of them in order that we can once more find the experience of religion in all of its purity and power.

Sin occurs when man tries to live by himself, isolated from the universe and his fellow men. He lives for his own selfish interest, but in so living he finds that he is miserable. This misery of man in his isolation is proof, to Schleiermacher, of man's oneness with God. It can be overcome only when one loses himself in the service of God and man.

Because sin separates man from God and his fellow man, God sends a mediator in Jesus Christ. The uniqueness of Christ is not to be found, for Schleiermacher, in some metaphysical doctrine about Jesus or in some miraculous origin such as the Virgin Birth. The real miracle is Jesus himself. In Jesus we find a man who had the sense of God-consciousness to a supreme degree; where we all have flashes of God, he had complete knowledge. Where we give fitful obedience, he gave complete obedience. Jesus, as the God-filled man, was a great pioneer in the realm of the spirit and morals.

Because Jesus has the full and complete knowledge of God, he is able to communicate consciousness of God to others. Through Jesus we can come into a vital and living relationship with God. The Church is the living witness to the fact that down through the centuries men have come to a vital God-consciousness through their contact with the life of Jesus. This leads to a true reunion with our fellow men in brotherly living.

In Schleiermacher religion found an answer to many of the problems of his age. For one thing, religion was made independent of philosophy and science. Religion, based on the individual's personal experience, had a realm of its own; it was its own proof; it bore its own validity. Furthermore, the center of religion is shifted from the Bible to the heart of the believer. Biblical criticism cannot harm Christianity, for the heart of the Bible message is that which it speaks to the individual, and it speaks even more clearly because the critics have enabled us to understand it.

Furthermore, other religions are no longer a problem; they too have their God-consciousness. The doctrines of religion may differ, but beneath them all there is the common experience. It is no wonder that Schleiermacher was hailed by many as the savior of religion, but much of his thought was obviously distasteful to orthodox Christianity.

Later in the nineteenth century, another school of thought began with another German thinker, Albrecht Ritschl (1822–1889). He was the great theologian of practicality. Religion must not be theoretical, he insisted. It must begin with the question, "What must I do to be saved?" but if that question means, "How can I go to heaven when I die?" then it is a theoretical question. To be saved means to live a new life, to be saved from sin, selfishness, fear, and guilt. Ritschl had no patience with metaphysics or with theological discussions that did not appear to him to have practical consequences. For example, he threw out Augustine's doctrine of original sin because it did not seem to him to deal with the practical question raised by the fact that some men are more sinful than others.

To be practical, Christianity must be built upon fact, so Ritschl welcomed the search for the historical Jesus. The great Christian fact is the impact that Jesus has made upon the Church through the centuries. God is not to be found in nature, which is red in tooth and claw and speaks ambiguously of its Creator. We find God instead in history, where movements arise dedicated to the values that make life meaningful. The task of theology is to turn men again to Jesus and remind them anew of what it means to follow him.

For Ritschl religion is based on value judgments and is to be sharply separated from science. Science tells us the facts, things as they are; but religion weighs the facts and deems some more valuable than others. The great fact about man is that, although he is a product of nature and evolution, he has a sense of values. We can explain this only if we interpret the universe as one which creates not only atoms and molecules but also values. For Ritschl God is not known intuitively, as for Schleiermacher, nor is God known by a rational inference from the world, as for the Deists. Instead, God is the necessary postulate to explain the sense of worth that man has.

Conflict between science and religion begins either when religion tries to make statements of fact or when science tries to make value judgments. When religion makes statements of fact, such as proclaiming that the evolutionary theory is wrong, the result is simply poor science. When science makes value judgments, such as saying that because man has evolved from the lower animals he is worth no more than the animals, the result is poor religion. Of course, Ritschl did not mean that science and religion should go off into two separate rooms and never speak to each other. Quite the contrary, the same man was to be both scientific and religious; religion was to use the facts of science, and science was to cherish the value judgments of religion. But it should be clear that religion and science are two basically different approaches to reality.

Applied to the problem of biblical criticism, this approach of Ritschl was very helpful to many in his generation. Biblical criticism takes the way of science; it decides what are the facts about authorship, date, and meaning of the biblical books. This is vital, for religion must be based upon fact. But the facts are not religion until they have been evaluated, and this cannot be performed by scientific criticism. If biblical criticism denies the occurrence of Jesus' miracles, his Virgin Birth, his preexistence, this does not make Jesus less valuable to us. Belief in the divinity of Jesus does not rest in any of these; it rests solely on the fact that he is the source of a value-creating movement; he has led men to find the God of values. That is, Jesus' life was the embodiment of such high ethical ideals and attainment that we are inspired to live as he did. Jesus is divine in the sense that he can do for us what God does; he makes us conscious of the highest in life. From Jesus' influence comes the Church, a value-creating community—the spearhead for building a society inspired by love, the Kingdom of God upon earth.

The man who did most to popularize Ritschl's views was Adolf von Harnack, a competent theologian in his own right and not simply the transmitter of another's views. His book *What Is Christianity?* (1901) was a record best seller. One of the reasons for its popularity was that it simplified Christianity. Harnack reduced Christianity to three affirmations. First, it affirmed belief in God the Father, his providence and goodness. Second, it affirmed faith in the divine sonship of man. Third, it affirmed faith in the infinite value of the human soul. He denied the miracles of Jesus and insisted that Jesus did not claim to be the Messiah or divine. It was Paul and later Greek thought that perverted Jesus' simple Gospel into the elaborate theology about Jesus that we find in later creeds. Hence the slogan that we must get back to the religion of Jesus, not the religion about Jesus.

The influence of Schleiermacher and Ritschl reached America late in the nineteenth century. Together they became the background of American liberalism. There had been prepared in America a movement to which these theologies could speak. From the time of Jonathan Edwards, America had begun to question the Calvinistic form of orthodoxy with which the country began. By the nineteenth century the

Unitarian movement was active. It denied the Trinity, the divinity of Jesus, and had staked religion to the findings of man's reason and faith in man's essential goodness.

Horace Bushnell, a Congregationalist, had criticized the orthodox doctrines of the atonement and popularized the idea of growing into Christianity. For many, the idea that one could become a Christian by training from childhood, instead of undergoing a soul-shaking conversion at some point in life, implied that there was no original sin. The child was born naturally good and would stay that way if raised properly.

Modern liberalism in America is the result of the various forces discussed in this chapter, joining with the native American forms of liberal thought.

From this chapter it is clear that by the close of the nineteenth century orthodoxy was "sore opprest" and "by schisms rent asunder." And, when speaking of the history of thought, we must not forget that the nineteenth century ends in 1914, not 1900. If we might describe the situation in the terminology of the boxing ring, we might picture it thus: At the close of the round, orthodoxy was hanging on the ropes and the crowd was cheering for the knockout. But orthodoxy was saved by the bell (the First World War) and when the next round opened, it came out fighting, with new vigor. Instead of retreating, it began to attack. It is still too early to decide if this new vigor is a permanent recovery or if it is a last desperate effort.

3

Fundamentalism and
Conservative Christianity:
The Defense of Orthodoxy

Most Americans are familiar with the term "fundamentalist" and many remember the theological battle early in this century between the fundamentalists and the liberals or modernists. All over the country, and in nearly every major denomination, there rose up men who were determined to protect the faith. To these dedicated men it was evident that the Christian Church had been infiltrated by subversives who would destroy Christianity from within.

The battle raged in Church assemblies, theological institutions, and the daily press. Young men about to be ordained to the ministry had to face a barrage of questions about their stand on the Virgin Birth, the bodily resurrection of Christ, blood atonement, and the infallibility of the Bible. We catch something of the flavor of the times in the following passage from an article in a secular magazine:

A few years ago we couldn't have imagined the United States eagerly awaiting the news from some church convention. There wasn't any news in a church convention. . . . The break came suddenly, about two years ago. What had happened no one seems to know; but the Virgin Birth presently began to run neck and neck with murder and politics for front page layouts, even in such newspapers as the *New York Times*. Ever since then religion has been the livest news there is.

A few years ago the country waited eagerly while the Presbyterians, assembled in Columbus, Ohio, actually took a ballot on the Virgin Birth. A little later the Associated Press and all the other news agencies of the nation were covering in World Series, play-by-play fashion an argument in a Tennessee courtroom on the all-important problem of where Cain's wife came from and whether God could have worked by the day before he invented the sun.

Now all eyes are beginning to turn toward New Orleans. The question at issue there is: Can a bishop think? Nobody seems to care particularly how the question is decided. The public isn't partisan; it is just eager for the news. For religion is news today, and no mistake.[1]

The term "fundamentalist" seems to have been used first by Dr. C. C. Laws, editor of the Baptist *Watchman-Examiner*. It implied that this view expressed the fundamentals of the Christian faith, the irreducible minimum of belief without which one

---

[1] Charles E. Wood, "Religion Becomes News," *The Nation*, Vol. 121, August 19, 1925, p. 204.

could not be Christian. Many representatives of this school were unhappy about the title, preferring the term "conservative Christianity" or even just "Christianity." John Gresham Machen complained that he saw no reason why that which had been known through history quite simply as Christianity should suddenly become another "ism."

During the first twenty-five years of the century, the fundamentalists were active in most Protestant denominations. They were on the offensive and attempted to root all liberals out of Church offices. Successful attacks were made on professors in theological seminaries, upon students who were about to be ordained, and even upon ordained clergymen. One of the better known cases involved Harry Emerson Fosdick, who was forced to leave the Presbyterian Church and return to his own denomination, the Baptist.

As time passed, liberals began to win more and more of the battles. The leading seminaries became the centers of liberalism, and fundamentalists either withdrew in discomfort or, upon retirement, were replaced by liberals. In a sense, if you want a date for the end of the fundamentalist-liberal controversy, it came in 1929. In that year Machen failed in his opposition to a reorganization of Princeton Seminary, where he taught. As a result he resigned and helped to found Westminster Seminary in Philadelphia. A second defeat came for Machen when he and other conservative Presbyterians founded an independent mission board. The Presbyterian Church ordered the dismantling of the organization, and the order was fought through the Church courts. Finally, in 1936, the General Assembly ruled against the independent board, and when its members refused to obey they were expelled. Machen and the others founded a new denomination, the Presbyterian Church of America. In short, by the thirties it was the fundamentalists, not the liberals, who were finding it necessary to leave churches and seminaries.

When one speaks of the end of the fundamentalist-liberal controversy, it does not mean that the fundamentalists disappeared. It does mean that the active battles died away. By the end of the thirties the liberals, as we shall see, were fighting for their lives on another front. On the other hand, the fundamentalists were often fighting among themselves and had little time to continue the attack upon liberalism. The pattern had been set so that liberals were found in one congregation and fundamentalists in another. Frequently, separate seminaries, one liberal and one fundamentalist, supplied ministers to the congregations even when they were of the same denomination. A large number of fundamentalists found their spiritual home among smaller sects where, unrestrained by scholarship, they became lost in a maze of esoteric emotional extravagances. Several of these groups have banded into the American Council of Christian Churches, which periodically makes headlines by calling the National Council of Churches a Communist front.

Rejected by most major denominations, torn by internal divisions, it appeared that fundamentalism was theologically dead by the time of the Second World

War. It remained a powerful force in the total life of the Church and the parish pastor often found that his congregation was torn by the old controversy, but theologians generally felt that fundamentalism had ceased to be of theological interest. In the late forties, however, there was a renaissance of scholarship in fundamentalist circles and a new conservative theology began to arise from the ashes of the older movement.

Typical of this renaissance was E. J. Carnell, professor of apologetics at Fuller Theological Seminary. He graduated from Wheaton College and Westminster Seminary, both strongholds of conservative Christianity. He took his doctoral degree, however, from Harvard Divinity School, a strong outpost of liberalism. He joined both the American Philosophical Association and the American Academy of Religion, neither of which can be suspected of fundamentalism. He wrote books on Reinhold Niebuhr and Soren Kierkegaard as well as several books which made rational and philosophical defenses of conservative Christianity. In the spring of 1967 he died suddenly at the age of forty-seven. His death was a serious loss to the conservative movement, but in the last two decades a host of younger men have made intellectual pilgrimages similar to that of Carnell so that his work will be continued.

With this theological renaissance of conservatism it has become necessary to distinguish between fundamentalists and conservatives. The new conservative theologians feel a deep kinship with their fundamentalist fathers and believe that they are speaking for

the best in the fundamentalist tradition. They find
their intellectual inspiration, however, in men like
Machen who were never happy with the term fundamentalist. They are keenly aware of errors in the fundamentalist approach to science and other modern
developments. This group has found an effective
evangelist in Billy Graham, who insists on conducting
his evangelical campaigns with ecumenical support
that transcends the boundaries of conservatism. The
journal *Christianity Today* presents the conservative
position to a wide circle of readers among both the
clergy and the laity. Conservative denominations have
combined with each other to form the National Association of Evangelicals. It should now be apparent
that, from the beginning, the term fundamentalism
was used to describe men who took quite dissimilar
approaches. For many years the threat of a common
enemy drove these men together, but in recent years
they have grown further apart. Within the fundamentalist movement there were always theologians who
were determined to defend orthodoxy with the best
scholarship available. They were suspicious of broad-
side attacks upon science or biblical criticism. They
were prepared to meet liberal scholarship on its own
ground. It is from these theologians that modern conservatism has come. The other group of fundamentalists were deeply suspicious of scholarship as such
and they put more emphasis upon the experience of
conversion than upon correct doctrine. In recent years
this second group has reserved its sharpest attacks
for the new conservative scholarship, in which it finds
the most dangerous form of modernism today.

The terms fundamentalist or conservative are not easy to define. Usually these terms are applied to anyone who believes in the verbal inspiration of the Bible, that is, the belief that the words of the Bible are the direct and errorless words of God. Yet, on closer inspection, it becomes clear that neither fundamentalist nor conservative was primarily interested in taking the Bible as the literal infallible word of God. Their primary interest was in the defense of orthodox Christianity. To meet the challenge to orthodoxy that we portrayed in the last chapter, these men chose to make the doctrine of the errorless Bible the first line of defense.

In our discussion of orthodoxy we had little to say about the doctrine of revelation, that is, the doctrine of how God makes himself known to man. That is because there is no such orthodox doctrine in the sense in which there is an orthodox doctrine of the Trinity. There is in all orthodoxy the faith that God has revealed himself, particularly in the events recorded in the Bible. This special revelation begins with the choosing of the Jews and culminates in the man Jesus. But there has been no final agreement on how God is revealed in the Bible or in what form it is an inspired book. In fact these are questions which did not become burning issues until the twentieth century.

In the pre-Reformation Church there were differences of opinion without any sharp conflict. Men like Augustine valued some parts of the Bible more than others, implying that there was a standard by which to test revelation within the Bible itself. Some thinkers, like Origen, interpreted the Bible allegorically, paying little attention to the literal meaning of its passages. Others, like Occam, had quite a literalistic point of view, the Bible being for them a divinely dictated law.

One of the most radical aspects of Luther's thinking was his handling of the Bible. He called Protestants back to the authority of the Bible over and above the authority of the pope and the Church. In the light of this we can appreciate the prophetic daring with which he treated the Bible. For Luther the Bible was not literally true from cover to cover nor were all parts of equal value. He found that there was in the Bible itself a criterion by which the whole could be judged. That criterion was the message of salvation by grace through faith which is spoken through Christ to the heart of the believer. In light of this criterion he started a movement that resulted in dropping from the Protestant Bible the so-called Apocryphal books which are still in the Catholic Bible. He questioned whether the books of Esther and Revelation should be in the Bible. He did not place much value on James' Epistle. He recognized that some of the forecasts of the prophets were in error, so that the Bible is by no means infallibly correct in all details. He even conceded that another New Testament could be written if anyone were as completely dedicated to the Holy Spirit as were the biblical writers.

These were brave attitudes in Luther, and it is not surprising to find that his followers and even Luther himself often retreated from them. As time passed, the Protestants felt more and more need of authority. Rome boasted that it had one voice of unquestionable authority while Protestantism had many conflicting voices. The sixteenth and seventeenth centuries were centuries of authoritarianism; the authorities of the divine-right kings clashed with one another and with the authority of an infallible pope. It is not difficult to understand why Protestants met authority with authority, and when Protestants used authority it had to be the authority of the Bible. But if the Bible is the authority by which you vanquish king and pope, you cannot treat the Bible as freely as did Luther. To protect their authority the Protestants claimed that the Bible was the only infallible authority and, unlike that of pope and king, the literal word of God. Every word in the Bible was, they claimed, dictated by God to the men who wrote it. One Protestant, A. Polanus, went so far as to insist that even the punctuation of the Bible was inspired and hence without error. It is this tradition which was inherited by fundamentalism.

To the fundamentalist this doctrine became the first defense against error. If one began by doubting any statement of the Bible, he had started down the slippery slope that, the fundamentalist believed, would lead to the denial of God and the divinity of Jesus, the loss of certainty of salvation and finally the loss of ethics. The fundamentalist sees a "creeping humanism," the creeping in of ideas that will finally leave man without God, religion, or morality. The fact that people have appeared in the modern world who are without God, religion, or morality spurred the fundamentalist in his zeal to protect the doctrine of the infallible Bible.

The heart of fundamentalism is in its concern for salvation. The only really important question is, "Have you been saved?" Because man is helpless to save himself, God must act. This helplessness if due to the fall of Adam, which caused sin in the world, a sin that is inherited by all men. Man is born with the guilt of Adam upon his soul, and he has a flaw in his character which leads him to sin. This sinful creature can do no act which can please God and is hence doomed to everlasting punishment in Hell unless God does something for him.

God is a God of love, mercy, and justice. The liberals, says the fundamentalist, overlook God's judgment and thus the love of God becomes pure sentimentality in their teaching. It would be unjust for God to forgive sins lightly and let bygones be bygones while the consequences of a man's sin live on and continue to injure others. Man has sinned and, in a moral universe, he ought to pay for his sin. Therefore, in his love and mercy, God sent his only begotten Son into the world. Jesus led a sinless life and did not deserve to die, but he voluntarily accepted death in order that he might save men. His death becomes a substitutionary atonement. He suffered the penalties of man's sin in order that the justice of God might be appeased and man allowed to go free. Jesus' blood was shed to wash away man's sin just as, in the Old Testament, the blood of animals was shed in the sacrificial rituals. The death of Christ does not save a man, however, unless he accepts Christ as the Son of God. The man who accepts Christ is assured of heaven and receives the grace of God as a power that enables him to overcome sin in his earthly life.

The miracles are the seals by which God proved his activity and presence to men. We know that Jesus was the Son of God because he was born of a Virgin, healed the sick, raised the dead, and was raised from the dead himself in a bodily form.

Most fundamentalists believe in the doctrine of the "pre-millennial" coming of Christ. This doctrine teaches that the Kingdom of God is not here now in the Church, as some groups have believed, nor is it a perfect society that man can build upon earth as many liberals believe. The Kingdom of God, the perfect society, awaits the Second Coming of Christ, when he will return upon the clouds and when history will end in catastrophe. Christ, having judged the living and the risen dead, will set up his Kingdom and rule for a thousand years, the millennium. At the end of that period there will be a final battle between the forces of God and Satan, and in the victory of God all the saints will be elevated to heaven for eternity while the damned will writhe in Hell.

This is God's plan of salvation, but how do we know that it is true? We certainly cannot know it if any man tells us, for no man's word is able to give us the assurance of salvation. Only God can say if it is true or not. If the Bible is the word of man, then we are still in our sins, without the assurance of salvation. But if the Bible is the Word of God, unclouded by errors or opinions of man, then we have an absolute assurance. Thus the doctrine of the infallible Bible is the protection for the Gospel message.

The doctrine of the infallibility of the Bible is frequently misunderstood. One hears it confidently refuted by the charge that it is a doctrine of mechanical inspiration and killing literalism. Again, it is refuted by pointing out that we have many manuscripts of the Bible and that often these differ from one another in the wording of certain passages. Some of the fundamentalists are vulnerable to such criticisms. We can find sects whose literal reading of the Scripture leads them to feel called to handle poisonous snakes or the like. Many of them refuse to consider the implications of the different manuscripts of the Bible. If we recall, however, that conservatives like Machen were excellent biblical scholars, we should realize that the conservative has an answer to such obvious criticisms.

Machen and like-minded conservatives assert that only the original manuscript of the Bible, as first inspired by God, was free from error. They make no claim that any edition of the Bible that we have today is without error. In fact, conservatives have done much work in biblical scholarship to restore the best text of the Bible. Although fanatical fundamentalists, believing the King James Version of the Bible to be infallible, have burned the Revised Standard Version, most conservatives advise their people to read the R.S.V. and other new translations. These conservatives believe that the original text of the Bible, which was free from error, has been lost because God knew that man would worship it as he has worshiped other religious relics. The men who copied the Bible made errors, which explains the differences in the manuscripts of the Bible, but God kept them from the kind of errors that would have hindered salvation. E. J. Carnell quotes the Introduction to the Revised Standard New Testament in which a group of nonconservative scholars concede that no manuscripts have been found that would change any doctrine of the Christian faith. This, says Carnell, is all that any conservative needs.

It is unfair to charge the conservative with being a literalist. He is not required to lop off his right hand or pluck out his eye because Jesus told men to do this. The conservative understands that the Bible sometimes speaks in poetic or allegorical language. He does not follow the literal words of Scripture; he follows the "natural" meaning. Where the Bible obviously means to be taken literally, he does so. Thus he believes in the bodily resurrection of Jesus because one cannot read the accounts without realizing that they say quite literally that Jesus arose in his body. But the conservative is not required to suppose that Isaiah saw the hills leaping and clapping their hands. The inspired word of God may be poetry as well as prose, and as such it is to be interpreted in its natural sense.

Having made such concessions, it may seem that the conservative is not so different from the liberal. The basic difference, however, is found when we consider the reaction to higher criticism. The lower criticism of the Bible is an area in which the conservative gladly works. In fact, he has greater concern than the liberal in finding the manuscripts that take us back most closely to the original version of the Bible.

Higher criticism is, however, a different matter. Fundamentalists reject all higher criticism as the work of the devil. Conservatives are not opposed to higher criticism in principle, but they do believe that liberal higher critics have fallen into error because of certain presuppositions with which they work. In the first place, charges the conservative, the liberal higher critic presupposes that the Bible is just another ancient book and that it does not require a special method to be understood. Failing to take the Bible on its own terms as a special revelation, the higher critic naturally misinterprets it. In the second place, says the conservative, the liberal higher critic presupposes a world view which is, in fact, without proof. According to this world view, no event can have occurred if it is not explainable in terms of our contemporary understanding of the world and man.

Because the higher critic has presuppositions and a world view which are unproved and which are often held unconsciously, he searches for the naturalistic causes of the Bible. As a result the higher critic distorts the Bible. For example, says the conservative, the higher critic has not disproved the possibility of miracles. Nor has he analyzed the biblical narratives and found them self-contradictory or innately irrational. He has not produced historical evidence which could cast doubt on the claim that Jesus performed miracles or rose from the dead. But the liberal critic has no room for miracles in his world view; they are distasteful to him. So he turns his imagination loose and works out ingenious theories to explain what really happened in place of the miracle. His attitude is neither critical nor scientific; it is based upon a dogmatic faith. The conservative believes that it is he who is really scientific here and not the liberal critic, for he does not, like the critic, presuppose that miracles are impossible. He looks at the facts with an open mind and finds evidence that miracles have happened.

In short, as the conservative sees it, what divides him from the liberal higher critic is not that one believes and the other doubts that Moses wrote the first five books of the Bible. Nor is the difference that one accepts the Bible as reliable history and the other questions it. In fact there is room among conservatives for different opinions on these points. The real difference lies in two totally different world views. The liberal higher critic, charges the conservative, assumes that the world is a self-contained unity that can be fully comprehended by man's intellect. He has no room for special revelation or for anything that might be called the interference of God with his creation. In short, he denies the reality of the supernatural; nature is all and explains all. The conservative accepts the reality of the supernatural God and of God's supernatural intervention among men. The world owes its being to the fact of God's creation. If the Creator chooses to act with his creative power again within the world to give a special revelation of himself or to perform miracles, then the truly reasonable man will accept this fact and not close his mind to it.

There is a widespread tendency to write off all fundamentalists and conservatives as irrationalists. Again, among the fundamentalists we can find examples of irrationalism, but we find that the conservative is not touched by such a description. It would be more correct to describe conservatism as rationalism within Christianity. No religious movement places more emphasis upon a rational faith than it. The defenders of conservatism gladly take their case into the arena of logic and reason because they believe that it is precisely here that they have their best case. For example,

E. J. Carnell, in his book *An Introduction to Christian Apologetics*, spends 350 pages in presenting a closely reasoned argument distinguished by coherency and ability to explain the facts. He reveals a knowledge of modern philosophy, science, and nonconservative theology. He attacks every effort to shield religion from the responsibility of defending itself rationally. He will not allow it to hide behind the intuitions of mysticism or feeling with Schleiermacher, nor will he allow it to express itself in contradictory paradoxes. He has only one reason for accepting conservative Christianity: it explains all of the facts of existence more coherently than any alternative philosophy. One may not agree with the arguments of this book, but one cannot call it obscurantist or irrational.

Carl Henry, editor of *Christianity Today,* is continually deploring the lack of respect for reason in contemporary non-conservative theology. He is confident that reason can demonstrate that God exists, the Bible is reliable history, and the Christian faith is true. Where modern theologians have denied this, he charges that they have opened Christianity to wishful thinking and made it vulnerable to its critics. Non-conservative theologians who conceded that they had no rational proof of God's existence and that they could not historically confirm the life of Jesus are followed, quite naturally, by theologians who declare that God is dead.

Although Carnell and Henry represent contemporary conservatism, their intellectual fathers had the same respect for reason. Machen, writing during the twenties, found the great weakness of liberalism to be its irrationalism and anti-intellectualism. Liberals, said Machen, argue that religion is an inexpressible experience, that the intellectual expression of it can only be symbolic, and thus the best way to make oneself unpopular in theology is to demand that people define the terms they use so blithely. Liberals toss around words like "God," "atonement," "redemption," and "Christianity," but refuse to define them so that they will mean the same thing for all people.

Liberals are obscurantists because they disparage the teaching of doctrine. The liberal says that he is only interested in applying Christianity to life. But, asks Machen, how can you apply something unless you know what it is? Yet, to know what Christianity is, you have to think about it; you have to consider its doctrines; in short, you need the theology which the liberal boasts that he ignores. This liberal disdain for theology is an excuse for shallow thinking or, worse still, for no thinking.

Furthermore, charged Machen, the liberal is anti-intellectual because of his habit of reading into the Bible what he wants to find there rather than seeing what really is there. The "Jesus of history" about which the liberal speaks a great deal is not the Jesus who is plainly evident in the Gospels, but the Jesus whom the liberals would like to find. The liberal wants a Jesus who is only a man and not the Son of God, and at the same time he accepts Jesus as the greatest moral and religious teacher. Could anything be more illogical? If Jesus was not and is not the Son of God, insists Machen, then he is the very reverse of a reliable teacher of ethics. For Jesus claimed to be divine; he claimed to have authority over men; he claimed to do that which only God can do—forgive sins; he claimed to be the Messiah, foretelling that he would return on the clouds of heaven; he asserted that he was the Way, the Truth, and the Life. If Jesus were only a man and claimed these things, he cannot be our example, for he was either a madman or a charlatan. Either way, it is irrational to honor him as a great ethical teacher. Yet this is typical of the failure of the liberal to be rational, to face the facts as they are not as he would like them to be.

In short, at the time when liberals were hailing themselves as the defenders of reason and of rational religion, this scholarly conservative arose to charge that it is liberalism which has betrayed reason. One may argue that there are flaws in the details of the conservative's argument, that he takes all of the mystery out of religion and makes it prosaically rational, but one cannot argue that conservatism is irrational.

One reason that conservatives and fundamentalists are thought to be irrational is because of the obscurantist battle waged against the theory of evolution in the name of fundamentalism. The term fundamentalism is still closely associated in the minds of men with the Tennessee law banning the teaching of evolution and the Scopes trial that resulted from it. But no system of thought can be judged by what fanatics do in its name. There are fundamentalists who condemn all science as being of the devil but conservatives have labored to relate the Bible and science.

In one of his first works Carnell presented a position

which he called Threshold Evolution. He points out that the Bible does not say that God created each individual species in the form that we know it today. Rather, God created each creature "after their kind," such as "herbs yielding seed" or "creeping things." Within each "kind" there are numerous species and these may have evolved from out of the basic "kind." What science cannot show is that one "kind" ever evolves from another. Here biology speaks of missing links or mutations, but it has no definite facts to work with. This "Threshold Evolution" can explain all of the facts known to science as adequately as any alternative theory. It enables the conservative to believe that man is the result of a special creation of God and that he did not evolve from lesser animals, for humans were one of the originally created "kinds." Since Carnell's work appeared a number of conservatives have attempted to show that evolution and the conservative view of the Bible are not incompatible.

The concern of the conservatives to be related positively to modern science has resulted in a group known as the American Science Affiliation. To be a member of this group a man must have a doctorate degree in one of the sciences. The members pledge themselves to the faith that the infallible Bible and true science cannot contradict each other. Several writings have come from this group to prove their point.

Conservatives have always been sensitive to the charge that they are narrow-minded obscurantists because of their efforts to rid the churches of those who do not agree with them. Machen attempted to answer this charge. Again he turned the liberal charge against the liberal. Narrow-mindedness, he insisted, does not consist in devotion to certain convictions or in rejection of others. That man is narrow-minded who rejects another man's convictions without trying to understand them. The liberal is continually saying, "Let us be broad-minded and unite in the same churches, for our doctrinal differences are mere trifles." But, points out Machen, it is of the very essence of conservative Christianity to regard doctrinal issues as matters of supreme importance. It is not narrow-minded either to believe or to reject the doctrine of the substitutionary death of Jesus for our sins. But it is the height of narrow-mindedness to ask, as the liberal asks, that a man who believes it should pretend that it is a trifle. If the liberal were truly broad-minded, that is, if he truly tried to understand the other's position and appreciate it, even if he could not agree with it, then he would see that his plea for union is a plea upon the liberal's terms. The liberal is, in effect, asking for unconditional surrender on the part of the conservative.

On the question of free speech, Machen argues that he has no desire that the liberal should not be free to hold and to spread his opinions. In fact, Machen concedes, the liberal may be a better Christian in the eyes of God than the conservative. Nevertheless, insists Machen, the Christian churches do have their creeds. A liberal may not agree with them; that is his right and privilege. He may think the creeds wrong or he may think that it is wrong to have any kind of creed. But if this is the case, honesty demands that the liberal go elsewhere to spread his views. There are churches that will welcome his ideas. Why does he ask to be supported by a church with which he disagrees? How can he honestly ask that a church support him while he undermines the doctrines upon which the church is built?

Conservatives are not persuaded that it is a violation of academic freedom if a Christian seminary limits what its professors may teach. Where is there a law school that would permit one of its professors to advocate the overthrow of the American Constitution? How many medical schools would retain a professor who preached the tenets of Christian Science? Are there many departments of biology that would permit a professor to reject the theory of evolution? Why should a seminary be so different that it dare not discharge a professor who teaches that God is dead or otherwise undermines the faith he has sworn to uphold?

As I have pointed out, by the time of the Second World War most nonconservative theologians assumed that fundamentalist or conservative theology did not need to be taken seriously. Unfortunately, it was felt that the movement still had a following in the churches, but that it could no longer be considered a live option for theology. When I wrote the first edition of this book, I prophesied that this might be changed by the rise of the new conservative theologians. I received more criticism for my chapter on conservatism than for any other part of that edition. Nonconservatives criticized me for presenting fundamentalists and conservatives too favorably. I had helped to preserve the "myth" that conservatism was still a live option for modern men.

As I revise this chapter I find that in the years since first I wrote it, the conservatives have moved further than I had anticipated. Far from dying out, various opinion polls indicate that the conservatives speak for a larger number of Protestant clergy and laity than does any other theological position. Conservatives are keen students of nonconservative theology and are willing to learn from it. Nonconservatives are less willing to read and much less willing to learn from the conservatives. Although the fundamentalist-liberal controversy is past history, its bitterness still seems to be a potent factor in American church life. Perhaps someday the ecumenical movement will become broad enough to include the conservatives.

4

Liberalism: The Remaking
of Orthodoxy

The term "liberalism," or "modernism," is difficult to define. For one thing, it became popular during the days of the fundamentalist-liberal conflict when anyone who was not a fundamentalist was, by definition, a liberal or a modernist. The latter two terms are used synonymously despite attempts to distinguish them. A further problem with definition is that liberalism is, by its very nature, such that there will be within it a great many diverse positions.

Despite the varieties of liberalism it did mean, for the majority of its defenders in the early years of this century, a reconstruction of orthodox Christianity. Although the fundamentalists saw the liberals as subversives of the faith, liberals saw themselves as the saviors of the essence of Christianity. For the liberal, it was the fundamentalist who was destroying Christianity by forcing it into the molds of the past and making it impossible for any intelligent man to hold it. Typical of the attitude of liberals was the oft-quoted statement of Fosdick that, for him, it was not a question of new theology or old but a question of new theology or no theology.

If we are to understand liberalism we must realize

that it has two elements. There is first of all the method of liberalism, a method that means liberals probably will come to somewhat different conclusions. There is, in addition, a body of thought which has grown up as typical of liberals.

The method of liberalism includes the attempt to modernize Christian theology. The world, liberals argue, has changed radically since the early creeds of Christendom were formulated; this makes the creeds sound archaic and unreal to the modern man. We have to rethink Christianity in thought forms which the modern world can comprehend. Fosdick argued that we must express the essence of Christianity, its "abiding experiences," but that we must not identify these with the "changing categories" in which they have been expressed in the past. For example, says Fosdick, an abiding experience of Christianity has been its conviction that God will triumph over evil. This has been traditionally pictured in the category of Christ's Second Coming on the clouds to destroy evil and set up the good. We can no longer retain this outworn category but we can still believe the truth which this ancient thought form was trying to express. We can continue to work in the faith that, through his devoted followers, God is now building his Kingdom and that there will be a renewing of our life, individual and social, to bring it into conformity with the will of God. The essence of the faith is thus retained, argues Fosdick, while the thought form in which it was once clothed has been abandoned.

A second aspect of the method of liberalism is its refusal to accept religious belief on authority alone.

Instead, it insists that all beliefs must pass the bar of reason and experience. Man's mind is capable of thinking God's thoughts after him. Man's intuitions and reason are the best clues that we have to the nature of God. The mind must be kept open to all truth, regardless of from whence it comes. This means that the liberal must have an open mind; no questions are closed. New facts may change the convictions that have become hallowed by custom and time. The liberal will venture forth into the unknown, firmly believing that all truth must be God's truth. In this spirit, the liberal accepts the higher criticism of the Bible and the theory of evolution. He refuses to have a religion that is afraid of truth or that tries to protect itself from critical examination.

It is evident that in so far as a man is a liberal on the basis of his method, it is possible to have liberals who draw diametrically opposed conclusions. It is not unimaginable that a man might follow the liberal method and come to a very conservative theological position. But liberalism came to be associated with certain conclusions as well as with the method described, and to continue our analysis of liberalism we must examine some of these.

Behind liberalism as it grew early in this century lay the philosophy of Absolute Idealism, coming from Hegel and Lotze but reinterpreted for America by Josiah Royce. Idealism is based on the belief that, if man is to have any faith in his knowledge, he must presuppose a rational structure to the world apart from his mind. Man's reasoning powers, his logic, and his a priori assumptions can only understand the world if the world acts in accordance with them. In other words, we can only trust our minds if the world is ultimately based on mind or reason. Idealism thus came to interpret all reality as the manifestation of a divine mind. Idealism seemed very appealing to many Christians because it attacked all philosophies of materialism.

Idealists like Royce and Hegel had made Christian terminology an inherent part of their systems. But to these men the Christian doctrines were only symbols of rational truths known to man's reason. Thus the divinity of Jesus was a symbolic statement for the fact that all men have a divine aspect to their natures. The basic concept of the Bible, which is that God has revealed himself in certain events of history, was considered by the idealists as naïve and pre-philosophical.

Idealism was an optimistic philosophy. It believed that the world was inherently rational and that reason was slowly overcoming the irrational. Good, it believed, was more basic than evil, so that the victory of goodness was ultimately assured. Sometimes this was identified with Christian belief in the Kingdom of God or, as Royce called it, the "Beloved Community."

Liberalism seldom capitulated completely to idealistic philosophy because the liberal theologians could not forget the Bible. But the liberals did draw heavily upon idealistic thinking. One of the most important ideas drawn from idealism was that of the immanence of God. Here we must examine some technical theological terms—"immanence" and "transcendence." Immanence implies an idea of God dwelling in the world and working through nature. Extreme immanence is pantheism, which says that God is the world and the world is God. Such pantheism appears in several of the idealistic philosophers but is rare among the liberals. Transcendence implies the reality of God apart from the world. Extreme transcendence is found in the Deists, for whom God is as separate from the world as the watchmaker is from his watch.

It is obvious that fundamentalism emphasizes transcendence without completely denying immanence. Its God is distinct from the world, and when he enters the world he comes in the form of miracle and special acts of revelation. Over against this, liberalism insists upon finding God in the whole of life and not in just a few spectacular events. God's way of doing things is the way of progressive change and natural law. Liberalism denies that some things are caused by natural forces and others by supernatural forces. The liberal sees God working in and through all that happens or is. Thus the Virgin Birth is important to fundamentalists as proof that in Christ the supernatural is at work. For the liberal the Virgin Birth is not only unnecessary but an embarrassment, for he finds God at work in the birth of every child.

Despite this emphasis upon immanence, most liberals retained the belief that God was transcendent as well as immanent. For example, Rufus Jones, in a passage which argues for the immanence of God, goes on to say that God is spirit and that it is the essence of spirit, even in the form in which we find it in man, to transcend itself. Therefore an immanent spiritual God must transcend the space-time universe. He is more than the universe but he is not radically separated from it.

In view of its belief in the immanent God, it is clear that liberalism would find the theory of evolution not simply a bitter pill to be swallowed by men who were determined to face all truth, but rather a vindication of the immanent view of God. Instead of suddenly breaking through the clouds to create the world, God had been working for ages slowly building through natural law the universe as we find it today. Some liberals would agree with the poet who said, "Some call it evolution, and others call it God."

Since God is at work in the world, and particularly at work in the spiritual life of man, God becomes, in liberalism, a humanized God. This does not mean that God becomes a glorified human being or that man becomes God, but it does mean that God is required to have the spiritual characteristics which we consider good in man. One liberal put it humorously when he said that, having been raised on a grim creed of Calvinistic predestination, it came to him as a great relief to find that God was at least as good as some of the elders in his church. Some liberals even worried over the term "Kingdom of God," which seemed to them to imply outworn feudalistic concepts. They suggested that we use a new term, "Democracy of God." They did not indicate whether God was to be the constitutional monarch or the elected president of this democracy. But it would be unfair to suggest that many liberals went to these extremes. Liberals did, however, insist that God owed certain things to man; man could demand certain inalienable rights even from God.

If God is found in the world process, it follows that we are not absolutely dependent upon special acts of revelation. Since one of the liberal's proofs of God is religious experience, and since such experience is not limited to Christianity, it is clear that other religions also have revelations. Man at his best is, in fact, a continuous revelation of God. Even those who do not recognize God may, in their devotion to high goals, be revelations of God's nature and will. There are differences among liberals at this point. Some, such as D. M. Edwards, would make all knowledge revelation so that scientific knowledge is as much revelation as any doctrine of Christianity. Other liberals are more cautious and believe that God can be found more clearly in Jesus and the Bible than he can be found in knowledge generally. All liberals agree, however, that revelation must be tested by reason and experience. Otherwise, they insist, how can we decide among the conflicting claims of revelation? Surely we are not to be left at the mercy of every fanatic who claims that he has a revelation from God. Many liberals would agree with J. S. Bixler that if some creeds reveal more about God than others, it is only because their prophets and wise men have made better use than others of the sense and wits that God gave them.

With this view of revelation in mind, it is not surprising to find that the liberal welcomed higher criticism of the Bible. Not only did the liberal believe that the Bible has no claim to preferential treatment among the books of man, but the liberal was happy to be freed from the need to apologize for the whole Bible as the infallible word of God. It was no longer necessary to defend a God who ordered the Israelites to kill their enemies to the last woman and child or who sent bears to eat children who poked fun at a prophet.

When the Bible is studied by higher criticism, the liberal believes that it becomes evident that God has revealed himself through an evolutionary process, just as he created the world. Beginning with primitive, bloodthirsty ideas, the Bible traces how the Jews slowly came to grasp the idea of a righteous God who can be served only by one who does justly, loves mercy, and walks humbly with his God. This progressive revelation of God finds its fulfillment in Jesus, where God is portrayed as the loving Father of all men.

The exact place of Jesus in liberal thought varies with the thinker. There are many liberals who look upon Jesus as divine and as a revelation of God. There are others who find in Jesus nothing more than one of the great leaders of religious and ethical thought. At no point is it more difficult to sum up liberalism in general. William Adams Brown, who for many years was a leading liberal spokesman, is perhaps typical. He argues that Jesus has been an authority for Christians in three ways. First, Jesus is the clearest illustration of the life which Christians desire to live and which they desire to see prevail in society. Jesus is an authority because he enables us to see more clearly than anyone else what the world would be like if everyone were loving. Second, Jesus exemplifies to his disciples the kind of spirit that must prevail if the life of love is ever to be realized in fact. We see through him that without the spirit of self-sacrifice, the good society can never be achieved. Lastly, Jesus symbolizes to his followers the resources on which they must rely if they are to overcome the obstacles which impede the life of love. Man needs aid from beyond himself. In Jesus we see one who was flooded by an inrush of divine love and who found that God was able to supply his every need. Thus he has become to his followers the symbol of what God is like and the channel whereby the love of God may find access to the spirits of men. This statement, while perhaps typical of the center of liberalism, would be criticized by some liberals as too radical and by others as too conservative.

Most liberals were keenly interested in the search for the historical Jesus. They felt that Christianity must be grounded upon the exact type of person that Jesus was. With this went a belief that a careful task of scholarship was needed to restore the true Jesus to view. This search for Jesus used varying slogans; sometimes it said, "Not Christ, but Jesus," signifying that "Christ" stood for a doctrine while "Jesus" represented the simple Galilean prophet. Another slogan was "The religion of Jesus, not the theology of Paul." Many liberals saw Paul as the chief culprit in hiding Jesus behind a smoke screen of theology.

There was far from complete agreement as to what kind of a man the real or historical Jesus was. But, in general, it was felt that he had been the teacher of a simple ethical religion, summed up primarily in the Fatherhood of God and the brotherhood of man. We saw this theme earlier in Harnack.

The fundamentalists cried in alarm that the liberals

were losing Jesus, the center of Christianity, and that the basic doctrine of his divinity was gone. The liberals answered that they were rediscovering Jesus. All that the fundamentalists had was the Christ of the "cradle, cross, and tomb." That is, liberals charged, the fundamentalist was only interested in the fact that the Son of God was born miraculously, that he died a substitutionary death, and that he rose from the grave. But the liberal wanted to bring the whole of Jesus' life once more before the gaze of Christians. The liberal charged that the fundamentalist was so concerned with theological doctrines about Jesus that he forgot to follow Jesus' teachings.

In general, it can be said that as the liberal tends to erase the line between knowledge and revelation, so he tends to erase the line between all men in general and Jesus in particular. All men are potentially the sons of God; Jesus is supreme and unique only in that he fulfilled the potentialities of all men more completely than any other. Those liberals who find meaning in the divinity of Jesus usually insist that it must no longer be interpreted in terms of the Nicene Creed, which says that Jesus was of the same substance as God; rather it must be interpreted in terms of character and spiritual unity. Jesus was one with God in that he completely lived the will of God in all things.

Liberals, as a whole, have usually denied the doctrine of original sin. This does not mean that liberals have been unaware of the fact that man is less than perfect; but the liberals have insisted that there is nothing radically wrong with human nature as such. There is no sharp cleavage between God and man, for man at his best is like God. Man can be won from sin by education and by holding before him the ideals of Jesus. Furthermore, there are degrees of sinfulness; a man can make progress in overcoming sin, and even if he does not reach perfection he can move in that direction.

Many unfair things have been written in recent years about the liberal's failure to understand the sinful depths of man's nature. True, there have been and still are liberals who can say with J. S. Bixler that sin is a theme for the esoteric poet and the disillusioned theologian who reaches into the past to find props for his outworn creed. Bixler also insists that there is an element of artificiality and make-believe in the use of the term "sin"; it is a concept into which we have to argue ourselves. But Bixler is not typical of liberalism.

Many liberals insisted that they were, in reality, taking sin more seriously than the fundamentalist. The fundamentalist, the liberal charges, condemns sin in general but neglects particular sins. The liberal insists that he has less to say about sin in general because he is concerned with the concrete sins such as corrupt politics, selfish exploitation, self-righteous dogmatism, racial discrimination, and so on. Walter Rauschenbusch pointed out, many years ago, that if you have a doctrine of the original fall of man it is a state of depravity so horrible that one is quite likely to pay scant attention to the contributions to sin which have been made by our more recent forefathers or by ourselves.

For all liberals ethics take a central place. At times

liberals fall back upon a pragmatic proof of their religion. The truth of religion is to be judged by whether it makes the world more of an ideal place in which to live.

This helps to explain the tendency of many liberals to disparage theology. Time, they feel, is wasted in theological debate that could be spent more profitably in ethical activity. Too much theology has no apparent ethical implications or consequences. The acid test of religion is not what a man believes but "Inasmuch as ye have done it unto one of the least of these . . ." For many liberals the philosophy or psychology of religion has taken the place of theology. E. S. Brightman, for example, heartily denied that he was a theologian; he said he was a philosopher with a particular interest in the philosophy of religion. As he saw it, there was no realm for theology that could not be handled by philosophy. This is an almost inevitable conclusion if revelation is either denied or identified with knowledge in general.

An important element of liberalism was the Social Gospel school. The exact relation of the Social Gospel to liberalism in general is difficult to analyze. On the one hand, it was the product of liberalism and most of its exponents were liberal theologians. On the other hand, it criticized liberalism for becoming identified with one class in society, the middle class, and it was from the Social Gospel concern that the radical criticism of liberalism was to come in men like Reinhold Niebuhr.

In one sense, the Social Gospel is as old as Christianity. Although from time to time there have been

Christians who fled from society and felt no need to make it Christian, the norm of Christian conduct has been to try to Christianize society. Medieval Catholicism certainly had a gospel for society and tried to build a Christian culture. Calvinism had a definite program for society, and it is no accident that all countries influenced strongly by Calvinism became democratic. The Reformation sects all looked in various ways toward the establishment of a Christian social order.

Nevertheless, there was a modern twist to the Social Gospel as it appeared among liberal Christians of the late nineteenth and early twentieth centuries. These men were in reaction against the individualistic gospel that had been presented by the more orthodox and fundamentalist groups. Social Gospel advocates insisted that it is not enough to preach a gospel that is simply fire insurance to save a man from Hell. There is no use saving individuals one by one when a corrupt social system is damning them by the thousands. The Social Gospel sees that man lives in a society and, to a great degree, is molded by his society. If the society is corrupt it will inevitably corrupt man. Quite frequently, the hope for a better earthly society replaced all active interest in a life after death.

The Social Gospel became convinced that by the "Kingdom of God" Jesus had meant neither an after-life nor a society upon earth which was to be set up by the supernatural act of God in the Second Coming of Christ. Rather, Jesus meant that society in which men are brothers, living in cooperation, love, and justice together. This ideal society is one that man himself, with the help of God, can build. In fact, man has already made many steps in this direction, such as the building of political democracy. At this point the Social Gospel joined hands with the secular faith in progress which was so strong in the first thirty years of this century. This did not mean that Social Gospelers were swept away with the naïve concept of an inevitable progress or that they thought it was a simple and easy task to build the perfect society. Rauschenbusch, who died in 1919, was one of the greatest exponents of this position, and he was well aware that there is a kingdom of evil, that is, a socially organized movement of evil. He saw that social progress can be retarded and lost. Although he threw himself wholeheartedly into the struggle of labor for a more fair and equitable income, he also looked forward to the time when labor, grown powerful, might have to be resisted in the name of the Kingdom.

Social Gospel thinkers did not have any one program for saving society. But they did tend to agree that there are fairly clear choices for the Christian to make in the economic, political, and social realms. Many of them identified the Christian social order with such things as democracy, socialism, the New Deal, or the cooperative movement.

Two problems in particular were close to the hearts of the Social Gospel thinkers—peace and race relations. Many repudiated all future wars, feeling that the First World War had proved their complete futility. Although others could not accept absolute pacifism, there was general agreement that war had to be abolished before the Kingdom of God could appear.

The League of Nations won their wholehearted support. It was this school of thought also which saw, long before it came to the view of the general public, that racial discrimination is a blot upon our claim to be Christian.

This, in brief outline, is the essence of the liberal movement, particularly as it appeared during the first thirty years of this century. This summary is not completely fair as a description of any particular liberal thinker, for, as is apparent, independence of thought was very dear to all liberals and such independence does not make it possible to describe all the variations of liberalism in the compass of one chapter. But if it is not adequate to describe any one thinker, it is, I believe, adequate to describe the mood and trends that were winning a victory over fundamentalism and gaining control of the leading seminaries and the official organs of leading denominations from 1900 to 1930.

When liberalism found that it had defeated fundamentalism in the sense which we pointed out in the last chapter, the liberals found that they were sharply divided among themselves. One can detect some three main trends in liberalism, although there are many individuals who cannot be fitted into any one of the three.

First, on the left wing of the liberals there grew up a group known as humanists. In 1933 this group published a manifesto which was clearly naturalistic in philosophy. That is, it denies the existence of God, immortality, and the supernatural in general. For these it substitutes faith in man and his capabilities.

Instead of looking beyond himself for help or dreaming of a life after death, man is to fulfill and develop his personality. This leads to the necessity of remaking society so that it will minister to the growth of man. All things are to be judged by the effect they have on man and his welfare.

The humanists claimed to be carrying the ideals of liberalism to their logical conclusions. Liberals had made God immanent; now humanism made him completely immanent: God is the world; God is man and his dreams. Liberals had appealed to religious experience; now humanists identify religion with experience. Wherever there is the experience of the integration of personality, there is religion. Liberals had emphasized ethics and judged religion by its ethical fruits; now religion is to be identified with ethics. Liberals had humanized the Bible; humanists see that it is a purely human book. Liberals emphasized the humanity of Jesus; humanists see him as a good man, a good teacher, although hampered by a pre-scientific view of the universe. But he is not to be preferred to other ethical teachers past and present. Liberalism, the humanist charged, had recognized the right of science to enter all fields, but somehow got cold feet when it was suggested that science could solve all problems. Liberalism, in short, is condemned for being a halfway reform; its supporters have seen the promised land from afar but have been afraid to enter it.

A second group of liberals emerged under the general heading of "The Empirical Philosophy of Religion." These men sought a religion that could be based squarely upon the scientific method. A. N. Wieman, a leader of one branch of this school, asserts that liberal theology wanted to be empirical but it allowed religious experience into its thought and this opened the door to unempirical subjectivity. Wieman wishes to have a God-centered instead of a man-centered theology. Thus he asserts that instead of looking within to our inner experience, we must look outside ourselves for the reality of God. He asserts that the time has come to quit arguing about the existence of God; God is to be defined so that his existence cannot be denied. Wieman has made several definitions of God, one of which is "God is that character of events to which man must adjust himself in order to attain the highest good and avoid the greatest evils."

Wieman does not believe that we can know about God except by experiment; we must live experimentally to find what values are suppported by the universe. For Wieman, God is a part of nature, that part upon which we depend for the production and preservation of human values. At first sight it may be asked, What is the difference between Wieman and the humanists, since both are naturalists in their philosophy? The difference is that Wieman is trying to find a source outside man which is the basis and background for man's values. The humanist, on the other hand, believes that values are the concern and product of man alone. Nature, apart from man, is indifferent to value.

Another wing of the empirical school has been that which is associated with Personalist philosophy and has found one of its leading exponents in E. S. Brightman. For Brightman, religion is to be based empirically on experience, but experience consists of all conscious life. To test the truth of religion one must test it by its coherence with all other knowledge and experience as a whole. While the philosopher of religion will consider experience that comes from mysticism, revelation, or other sources, each must finally be judged by reason.

Whereas Wieman's God is not personal, Brightman's is. Brightman comes to this conclusion by weighing various facts of experience and finding that the hypothesis of a personal God is the most coherent hypothesis to explain such facts. God is not a person, but is personal in the sense that he includes a rational will and is the source of human values. He is also personal in the sense that human beings may have a personal relationship with him.

The most unique aspect of Brightman's theory is that God is limited. Faced with the problem of evil, Brightman assumes that a completely good and a completely powerful God would not allow evil. Since he has evidence for believing God to be good, it follows that God cannot be all-powerful. The limiting element is within God himself, as an uncreated given aspect of his nature. Man is thus called to be a co-worker with God in the struggle against evil.

The third group of liberals included the majority of liberal churchmen. Each of the former positions represents a radical break with orthodox Christianity. The third type of liberalism is much closer to orthodoxy. It has been called Evangelical Liberalism in the sense that it retained the essential "evangel" or gospel of

Christianity. It is found in men like Harry Emerson Fosdick, W. A. Brown, Rufus Jones, and H. S. Coffin. These men were dedicated to reason, an open mind, and the currents of modernity, but they also were rooted firmly in the Bible and Christian tradition. They were certain of the reality of God, and while they preached his immanence they believed that he transcended the natural world. They found uniqueness in Jesus and the Christian religion and, if they could not go all the way with orthodox creeds, they could stand with the orthodox in accepting Jesus as Lord of their lives.

Rufus Jones was typical of this school. He was deeply interested in mysticism, by which he meant man's direct knowledge of God. God can be known by man as a spiritual power which is available to him. God is the resource beyond man from which man can draw strength. Man is thus a creature who lives in two environments, one earthly and one spiritual. The man who lives in the earthly environment alone, or at least who tries to do so, is not a full man; he is throttling his truest potentialities. The process of salvation is not away from normality but rather the attainment of completely normal spiritual health.

Jones's mysticism led to action. As Fosdick points out, Jones lived, rather than talked about, Christian conduct. He was, more than any other, responsible for founding the Friends Service Committee, whose works of relief and rehabilitation are of renown across the world.

For Jones the Bible was not an infallible book; there was a real human element in it and, as in all things human, there was error, triviality, and actual evil. But despite this, he asserted that there is a uniqueness about it. Through all of its human weakness, Jones could hear the Spirit of God speaking through the writers, speaking a word to his heart where God also spoke.

Jones feels that the arguments over whether Jesus was divine or human rest upon a mistaken conception of man. If man is completely alien to God, then it is difficult to see how Jesus could be both God and man. But if we believe that man is essentially related to God, created in his image, the problem becomes simple. In Jesus we find one in whom the divine possibilities of man have come to full growth. Because in Jesus a man gave himself completely to God, he becomes the one in whom we can see God. God, being a spirit, could not reveal himself in any complete way except through a person. It takes a person, dedicated totally to God, to show man what God is like. Christ is thus the great center of history; we do not know of what the universe is capable until we see what man becomes in Jesus. The greatest fact of history is that God broke into it through this unique person. But Jones is sure that if God broke into history here, it does not mean that he is absent from history at other times. God reveals that he is present in the whole of history and in the heart of every man.

In the position of this third group we find an attempt to keep the God of Jesus Christ and to keep Jesus as the revelation of God. It believes that Christianity can be enriched from many quarters, that all truth belongs to it. But it is not prepared to sacrifice

Christianity to the acids of modernity. This represents the meaning of liberalism to most liberals through the twenties and the thirties of this century. Yet it was a position that found itself under great stress, and it is not surprising that as liberalism rethought its position it was from this group that the reorganization came.

Liberalism, in the very moment of its triumph over fundamentalism, began to disintegrate. As early as 1934 Walter M. Horton, a liberal, could write, "Liberalism as a system of theology has collapsed." Horton went on to point out that even liberals hardly ever spoke or wrote without making some gibe at liberalism.

Horton, in pronouncing the demise of liberalism, insisted that there were values in it which must be maintained and preserved for the future, but, to do so, liberalism had to be remade. Ironically, liberalism's "abiding experiences" had to be put into new categories so that a new age could understand them. Liberalism had performed so well the task of fitting itself to the modern age that, when the age passed, a new generation came onto the scene for whom liberalism was as difficult to comprehend as fundamentalism had been for the previous generation. Some liberals abandoned liberalism completely and laid foundations for the neo-orthodoxy which we shall look at in the next chapter. Others, however, undertook the task of reworking liberalism and became known as "neo-liberals."

To understand neo-liberalism we must understand the reasons why liberalism declined in the thirties. Liberals found themselves between the humanists and the fundamentalists. It was disturbing to the liberals to find that the criticism from both sides was strangely similar. Both opponents insisted that the logic of liberalism ought to lead it to humanism. Humanists charged the liberals with cold feet: they were afraid to trust man and put their hope in human progress as their logic demanded. Fundamentalists had always insisted that this was the logical conclusion of liberalism. William Jennings Bryan had charged that liberalism was simply an anesthetic to put man to sleep while his belief in God was amputated.

During the calm, prosperous days of the twenties, the humanist argument had a tantalizing appeal. Man was rapidly solving the problems of the ages. Science, education, and man's organizational genius were doing what traditional religion had failed to do. Truly it seemed that all we needed was a little more faith in man and a little more effort. But in 1929 this faith crashed with the stock market. America began to learn what Europe already knew, that the twentieth century was not the dawn of Utopia. Faced with the proposition that their presuppositions led logically to humanism, liberals, instead of going humanist, reexamined their presuppositions.

More important in the decline of liberalism than the criticism either of humanist or of fundamentalist were the events of the century. The twentieth century opened as the century of promise, the century in which science, harnessed to the needs of man, was to banish all ills from the face of the earth. In fourteen years it brought the most bloody war known to man. America, isolated from that war, could still keep its optimism in the belief that it had been a war to end wars. Europe could not be so hopeful, and somewhere between 1914 and 1918 liberalism died in Europe. America at first could not understand the strange theology of Barth and Brunner that was born across the Atlantic, but after the depression of 1929 it commenced to search its own soul.

The depression had a deep influence upon America. The great industrial giant sprawled helplessly, unable to overcome the ridiculous problem of having produced too much. President Hoover kept promising prosperity around the corner, but it did not come. Roosevelt and his New Deal gave a spark of hope, but unemployment was not overcome until the threat of another war sent men to work again. In the meantime the totalitarian states had risen. At first Russian Communism could appear as one manifestation of the coming age of promise. But, by the middle of the thirties, it was seen as a reign of terror to all except those whose need of faith was so great that they had to believe that someone was triumphing over the problems that faced all nations. Then came World War II, the murder of six million Jews, atomic bombs, the cold war, Korea, and the ever-present threat of World War III. It is not strange that a theology born in the late nineteenth and early twentieth centuries would find that a change in its thinking was necessary.

The central character in Howard Spring's novel *Fame Is the Spur*, looking at the world of 1940 and thinking back over his long life, comments that the world of 1940 is drastically different from that in which he grew up. In the world of his youth "No good had seemed impossible," but now there was an age in which "No evil, no bestiality, no treason or treachery seemed incredible." Modern man began to feel lost, The word "anxiety" became a cornerstone of psychological thinking. Man sought to get the world back to normal, but those who knew history could only tell him that it was back to normal. The abnormal ages were those idyllic years when "No good had seemed impossible." What could the liberalism of the early twentieth century say to this modern man?

Liberals began to ask themselves some serious questions. If it is obvious to any rational man that the great need of our world is for brotherly living, why do not men live like brothers? We ought to love our neighbors as ourselves and thus put an end to war, economic injustice, racial discrimination, and other evils that now threaten to destroy man or make his life a nightmare. Why has man refused so consistently to follow the simple, rational way to salvation? It will not do to say that man has not been properly taught, for all cultures have emphasized these ideals. Can it be, liberals were forced to ask, that there is some truth in orthodoxy? Is man inherently sinful? Is there a radical weakness in man's nature which turns him from the self-evident way of his own salvation?

In the light of these questions, neo-liberals were forced to doubt that the real problem was to tell man how he ought to live. On the whole, man seems to know that. Is not the real problem how to remake man so that he can do what he ought? Was Paul perhaps presenting the true human situation when he said, "But how to perform that which is good I find not" (Rom. 7:18)? If this is the case, do we not need something more than a teacher of ethics in Jesus? Do we not need a savior who can release us from the bondage to sin? Neo-liberals had no simple answers to these questions, but they agonized over them.

The threat to liberalism did not come simply from the events of the time; there was also a reappraisal of many of the facts and theories upon which liberalism had built. For one thing, the idealistic philosophy went out of fashion and was replaced by analytical philosophy in Britain and America and by existentialism in Europe. Liberals, who had dedicated themselves to relating theology to current forms of thought, suddenly found themselves defending a philosophy that was out of date.

The Bible became a problem for liberals. For one thing, if the truth of the Bible is only that which we can experience in more modern categories, and which we can know by reason, why bother with the Bible at all? Why spend all the time in searching for the historical Jesus when he says nothing but love God and your neighbor, things which we can figure out for ourselves? Is there a hidden element of authoritarianism in the liberals who have renounced authoritarianism? Does a truth of reason gain more cogency when we find it in the Bible or spoken by Jesus? Why do we spend more time dissecting the Bible than the *Analects* of Confucius if there is nothing unique about the Christian faith?

This question became more pointed as the direction of biblical scholarship in the twentieth century became clear. We cannot say that archaeology and biblical criticism have proved the truth of orthodoxy, but in recent years they have given more comfort to the orthodox than to the liberal.

We can mention a few ways in which this is so. The liberal interpretation of the Old Testament was firmly grounded on the theory of Wellhausen, a nineteenth-century German scholar. This theory assumed that, by dating the writings of the Bible, we could reconstruct the history of how its ideas developed. In the light of this an evolution was found in the Bible from its early primitive beginnings in polytheism, up through stages to belief in one ethical God. This view was presented to the lay reader in Fosdick's well-known book *A Guide to Understanding the Bible*. But the trend of the times is indicated by the fact that a leading Swiss biblical scholar calls Fosdick's book "an obituary of last century's scholarship." It is now seen that Wellhausen was, to a large extent, rewriting history to fit Hegelian philosophy with its concept of evolutionary development. Archaeology makes it seem probable that Israel's monotheism goes back at least to Moses, a point completely denied by Wellhausen.

Liberalism, however, was disturbed most of all by the developments of biblical scholarship in the New Testament field. The nineteenth-century scholarship was analytic; it took the Bible to pieces and analyzed the parts. The result was a seeming conglomeration which lacked unity and enabled the liberal to set one part of the Bible against another, for example, Paul against Jesus. Twentieth-century scholarship, using the results of analysis, went on to synthesis, and discovered that the Bible in general and the New Testament in particular represented a unity.

The quest for the Jesus of history turned out to be a will-of-the-wisp. We have learned much from the efforts. Jesus stands forth much more clearly in all of his manhood, his beauty of character, and his moral power. But he is not the Galilean carpenter who taught a simple ethic for whom the liberals were hopefully searching. Instead, modern scholarship finds a man who was conscious of a heavenly destiny and who announced himself as God's chosen agent for the salvation of men. Paul's gospel about Jesus is not radically different from Jesus' gospel about himself.

As a consequence, Paul is no longer the villain in scholarly circles. He cannot be honestly portrayed as the perverter of the simple gospel that Jesus taught. The basis of Paul's gospel and the gospel of the earliest Church is now known to be identical. Paul is no longer seen as a Greek thinker who brought in concepts from the mystery religions; his background was Jewish and Christian.

Furthermore, John's Gospel, a stronghold of orthodoxy, can no longer be banished to the outer darkness of neglect by critical scholars. Recently discovered fragments of the Gospel prove that it was being circulated at the end of the first century, which is earlier than many scholars formerly thought that it was written. Scholars are no longer so dogmatically certain that it was not written by the disciple of Jesus. At certain points it is recognized as better history than the Synoptics.

A. M. Hunter summarizes the findings of New Testament scholarship in this century with this significant passage:

> Despite the aberrations and excesses of individual critics, the course of New Testament studies in the twentieth century has been mainly to make more sure the foundations on which our Christian faith is built, and to increase and deepen our conviction that a "new face" has been put upon life by the blessed thing that God did when he offered up his only begotten Son.[1]

In short, twentieth-century biblical scholarship has been far from supporting liberalism at crucial points. When liberals, at the turn of the century, threw in their lot with the biblical critics and swore to follow wheresoever truth led, they hardly bargained that they would be led back to orthodoxy.

Such, in brief outline, are some of the reasons why liberalism fell into difficulty. But if liberalism is true to its central method, if it is truly trying to mediate Christianity to the world in which it lives, and if it is ready to follow reason and experience, it ought to have the ability to adapt itself despite the blows that have fallen upon it. That is precisely what the neo-liberals tried to do.

The most decisive moment in the changing course of liberalism occurred one Sunday morning in 1935 when Harry Emerson Fosdick stood up to preach in his beautiful skyscraper church in New York. This man was the great symbol of liberalism. Reinhold

[1] A. M. Hunter, *Interpreting the New Testament, 1900–1950* (Philadelphia: The Westminster Press, 1951), p. 140.

Niebuhr has pointed out that he was that rare combination, a great preacher and a great theologian. For many years his voice brought the message of moderate liberalism over a nationwide radio hookup. His books were best sellers. Although Fosdick was never one of the most radical liberals, the fundamentalists quite rightly singled him out as their most dangerous enemy. Here was a man who had the ear of millions and who, in persuasive and beautiful language, was reasoning men into liberal Christianity. Humanists likewise saw in Fosdick the chief antagonist, the leader of liberals who refused to "follow their logic" to humanism.

Although ordained a Baptist, Fosdick was called to the First Presbyterian Church of New York. Presbyterian conservatives carried on a battle to have him replaced and finally passed a statement of faith which all non-Presbyterian ministers in Presbyterian congregations had to sign. Fosdick refused and went to the Park Avenue Baptist Church on the condition that it would be a creedless church, accepting all into membership who desired to enter. His congregation later built the present Riverside Church, one of the leading Protestant churches in the nation.

On the before-mentioned Sunday, in the midst of the depression, Fosdick dropped an unexpected depth charge into the sea of theology. His topic was "The Church Must Go Beyond Modernism." It was by no means the first storm warning to arise in liberalism, but when Fosdick, the unofficial general of the liberal army, spoke out, the change in liberalism became apparent. The fundamentalists shouted in glee and many a liberal felt betrayed by his leader. Neither attitude was justified. Fosdick had not ordered a retreat; he had laid the plans for a new attack.

Fosdick began that memorable sermon by insisting that the church had had to go modernist; he was not backing down. He told how a boy, fifty years earlier, had cried himself to sleep in terror lest he go to Hell, while his mother, out of patience with the religious teachings that had caused the fear, tried to comfort him. "That boy," said Fosdick, "is preaching to you this morning." Modernism was essential, claimed Fosdick, if men were not to have their intellect in the nineteenth century and their religion in the sixteenth.

But, necessary though modernism was, it was not enough. It aimed, quite rightly, to make religion speak to the times, but it had to do more than accommodate itself to the times or it would be shallow and transient. Fosdick found in particular four weaknesses in modernism.

In the first place, modernism had been excessively preoccupied with intellectualism. Its great goal had been to adjust Christian thinking so that a modern intellect could understand and accept it. Necessary as this was, it is no more than one of many problems. The deepest experiences of man's soul, whether in religion or elsewhere, are not just matters of the intellect. We are wise to use our heads; but rather than to approach problems head first we should do better to approach them heart first, conscience first, imagination first. Man is greater than his rational process, and to be preoccupied with the intellectual problem is to handle only a portion of man's life. Furthermore, the critical spiritual problems are no longer intellectual; they are moral. Can Christ meet the problem of sin in our personal and social lives? What our modern world needs is not so much souls intellectually adjusted to it as souls "morally maladjusted to it."

In the second place, modernism has been dangerously sentimental. This is due to the fact that the late nineteenth and early twentieth centuries to which modernism adjusted itself were buoyed up by the illusion of inevitable progress. Thus modernism had eliminated the idea of the moral judgment of God. Granted that the former horrors of theology had to be rejected, it was sentimentality, not realism, that supposed there was nothing to fear in God. Sin, personal and social, is real, insists Fosdick, just as our forefathers told us, and we can see that, as they told us, sin leads men and nations to damnation.

In the third place, modernism has watered down the concept of God; it has adjusted itself to a man-centered culture. God was relegated to an advisory capacity as a "kind of chairman of the board of sponsors of our highly successful human enterprise." It is necessary, said Fosdick, to turn again to theology, the problem of existence, the problem of what is eternally real. If the materialist is right and this world is nothing but matter and man is just the accidental result of the fact that the cooling off of the earth produced the necessary conditions for him, then it is ridiculous to find dignity or glory in him. The time has come to quit being apologetic; we must quit acting as if the highest compliment that could be paid to Almighty

God is to have a few scientists believe in him. Christianity has its own standing ground, the only one that can give hope to man: it proclaims that the eternally real is spiritual, that the highest in us comes from the deepest in the universe.

Finally, Fosdick charged, modernism has too commonly lost its ethical standing ground and its ability to launch a moral attack. It has become too well harmonized with the modern world. It is all very well to accommodate one's thought to astronomy and biology, but when one gets into the habit of accommodating and begins to adapt oneself to nationalism, imperialism, contemporary capitalism, and racialism, then it is dangerous.

Fosdick closed with a challenge. Modernism has won the battle it set out to win; the fundamentalists are now in the backwaters and the future of the Churches is with modernism if it will have it so. Therefore, let the modernist battle cry be, not "Accommodate yourself to the prevailing culture," but "Stand out from it and challenge it." We cannot harmonize Christ with modern culture, for Christ is a challenge to it.

I have summarized Fosdick's sermon at considerable length because it represents the basic tendencies in the neo-liberal movement. It had been preceded by many storm warnings. Liberals like Walter Horton and John Bennett were warning that liberalism had to change its ways if it was to speak to the modern man. Many of these liberals banded together under the slogan of "realism." The term "neo-liberalism" serves better, however, to indicate the organic relationship to liberalism that characterized these thinkers even in their reaction to its early twentieth-century forms. As Horton said, "Liberalisms perish, but liberalism remains."

The term "realism" implies that these liberals have abandoned idealistic philosophy. They are looking outside man, not within, for the clue to God. The subjective experiences of man are put second to man's knowledge of a reality apart from himself. God is no longer thought of in terms of a construct of man's mind, but as a factor in man's environment to which he must adjust himself.

In line with this, the neo-liberals have criticized the liberals for constructing God in terms of what they would like him to be, instead of searching for what God really is. Liberals had argued against attributing certain characteristics to God because they seemed immoral or, in short, because they did not fit into what the liberals wanted God to be. But, says the neo-liberal, we must adjust ourselves to what God is whether we like it or not. Instead of preaching only those doctrines that promise to be pragmatically useful to man in building a better world, we must preach those which are true.

Part of the realism of neo-liberals is their firm resolve to face all of the darkest and worst facts about the human situation. Elton Trueblood gives to one of his books a title that expresses their concern—*The Predicament of Modern Man*. Central to all neo-liberalism is the realization that man is in a predicament, that life is no simple success story, that the predicament calls for something more than fine-sound-ing ethical ideals. In a world like ours, as Herbert Wallace Schneider says, man "does not need to seek God, but finds himself driven to God."

Horton is forced to realize that God approaches man, as it were, with two hands. The one hand is open to woo us with love, but the other is a mailed fist which will crush our best laid schemes if they do not accord with his will. God longs to have us accept his loving approach, but when we do not we find that we are crushed with depression, war, psychological maladjustments, and the destruction of our civilization. The gulf between the two hands can only be bridged by Christ and his Church. Yet there is hope even in the mailed fist of God, for it assures that every evil system bears the seeds of its own destruction.

The realistic analysis of the predicament of man drives neo-liberalism to the realization that the orthodox doctrine of sin is, in many ways, more realistic than the liberal optimism about man. Shortly after the turn of the century, G. K. Chesterton, a Roman Catholic layman, chided the liberals that they had dropped the only doctrine of Christianity which could be empirically verified, the doctrine of original sin. Neo-liberals came to see the point. Without restoring the full Augustinian position, neo-liberals have recognized real truths in it.

The position of most neo-liberals would not be too different from that of John C. Bennett as he outlines it in his chapter of a book called *Liberal Theology*, edited by D. E. Roberts and H. P. Van Dusen. Bennett wishes to keep certain truths of liberalism. First, it recognized that man is essentially good as the creation of God. All men, not simply Adam before the fall, are created in the image of God. Man, as we find him, is not essentially evil but is "as a good thing spoiled." Augustine realized this, although some of his followers have forgotten it. Second, we must realize that man is also a finite child of nature, subject to the laws of nature. In light of this, Bennett cannot follow those orthodox thinkers who have supposed that man's impulses, such as sex, are basically evil. Man dies because he is an animal, not because he is a sinner. Third, man is a rational being, and rational living in the widest context is good living. Reason is our protection against false revelations. Fourth, man is free and responsible for his actions. Fifth, man can find his true self only in social relations. Loyal membership in communities is the major content of the good life.

But Bennett also accepts truths from the Augustinian tradition. First, there is the doctrine of sin. Sin cannot be defined simply as those choices which are made in the knowledge that they are sinful or opposed to the will of God. The real human problem is that we so easily deceive ourselves and thus persuade ourselves that our evil acts are really good. Second, we have to learn from Augustinianism that there is sin on every level of moral and spiritual growth. Every human good can be corrupted. In short, a perfect life is not humanly obtainable. Third, because of the foregoing, all Utopian hopes are illusory. The perfect social order cannot be built upon earth. This does not mean that there can be no changes for the better, but it does mean that progress will never be free from the danger of serious setbacks, and every reform will have its unexpected by-products of evil. We cannot assume that our achievements will lead to the Kingdom of God on earth. Fourth, we are led to recognize that repentance is a continuous necessity. Such repentance keeps us from self-righteousness and contempt for others in their sinfulness.

It is evident that neo-liberalism is unable to be as hopeful for solving man's dilemmas as was liberalism. It is not so sure that a particular social activity can be called Christian. Social Gospel liberals always knew that the present American capitalist system cannot be called Christian. Neo-liberals are willing to concede that it could not be replaced by a perfectly Christian system. This does not rob the neo-liberal of hope. He can still work for improvements in any social situation, but he is not led to expect unqualified success.

Likewise, the neo-liberal is increasingly convinced that society and man cannot be remade simply by education and science. The drag of self-centeredness in human nature is such that mere educational manipulation or scientific improvement cannot overcome it. Social reform must always make use of means of coercion as well as of persuasion. Religion must offer a power to change man's life as well as education in ethical ideals.

Inasmuch as God is no longer identified with man at his best, neo-liberals are ready to admit a need for some kind of mediator between God and man. Since we cannot find God by looking at man, God must reveal himself. Once more neo-liberals are turning to "Christ," not just the "Jesus of history." They have not come to any agreement upon what is meant by the divinity of Jesus, but they are increasingly aware that it must be taken seriously. Jesus is not just the best that man has accomplished; he is a gift of God to man. Georgia Harkness probably speaks for her fellow neo-liberals when she asserts that in this area we need convictions without dogmatism.

One of the significant aspects of neo-liberalism is its new sense of the importance of the Church. Since Fosdick called them to stand over against the world and not simply conform to it, neo-liberals have felt the need of a place to stand. Added to this has been the experience that the leaders of the movement have had in the ecumenical movement where they have seen the Protestant Church organizing itself and trying to understand itself.

Liberals in general had little concept of the Church. To many liberals the Churches were simply social organizations of men gathered together because of a common religious and ethical concern. The necessity of the Church was purely practical: men are able to do more when organized than as individuals alone. It is typical of liberalism to be prohetically critical of the Churches as they exist. Liberals criticized both the division of the Churches and their failure to live the teachings of Jesus.

Neo-liberals are dissatisfied with this liberal concept. They have not ceased to express the liberal critique of the condition of the Churches, but they have come to believe that there is a Church over and beyond the split denominations. It is a living society, begun in the work of Jesus and continuing that work through the ages. It is not just another social organization to be explained in sociological terms; it is a divine institution, founded by God. Walter M. Horton even goes so far as to say that as Christ had a divine and a human nature, so has the Church.

In the early nineteen forties, George Hammar, a Swedish theologian, made a survey of American theology and came to the conclusion that neo-liberalism was a highly unstable form. He called it a transitional theology which had broken from its liberal moorings but had not thrown in its lot with orthodoxy. Today it is apparent that the neo-liberals were unable to develop a school. Many of their followers turned to neo-orthodoxy. Leaders like Horton sought to develop an ecumenical theology that drew truth from various positions rather than trying to develop a particular school. John Bennett, perhaps the most capable of the neo-liberals, was never content to be stereotyped into any position. Most of his work in recent years has been in Christian ethics where he has sought to work out realistic Christian policies to meet the social, political, and international problems of the world.

Not many theologians today desire to bear the banner of liberalism. It could be said that liberal theology has passed from the scene. And yet, as we examine the following chapters, it will be evident that liberal themes continue to appear, and when we come to the chapter on contemporary trends (Chapter 11), we shall see a revival of several liberal themes. The term "liberal" may be in disfavor but the legacy of its thought is still a powerful force in theology.

5

Neo-Orthodoxy:

The Rediscovery of Orthodoxy

We have seen that liberal theology came under considerable criticism and a neo-liberal movement developed. There were, however, a number of theologians who went beyond neo-liberalism and became known as neo-orthodox. The term was always an unfortunate one. "Neo" implies the new and different; "orthodoxy" implies the old and traditional. One is reminded of an event in Canadian politics. After going out of power in the early thirties and losing several elections, the Conservative party decided that its name was a liability in a forward-looking and progressive-minded country. So it changed its name to "Progressive Conservative." This led a political opponent to write a satirical essay entitled "The Progressive Conservatives: Or How to Go Forward Backwards." Neo-orthodoxy seems to have the same implications. It is only fair, therefore, to point out that the name was not coined by representatives of the movement but by its opponents.

Despite its paradoxical flavor, neo-orthodoxy is a useful term to describe a trend that developed in theology. After the liberals had revolted against orthodoxy, a number of theologians began to find new relevance in many doctrines of orthodoxy such as sin, revelation through Christ, and salvation through grace. But, on the other hand, these theologians did not simply return to orthodoxy. A majority of the neo-orthodox began as liberals and this colored their thinking in two ways. On the one hand, certain aspects of liberalism lived on in them; they were as critical of fundamentalism as the liberals had been; they accepted biblical criticism in its most radical forms. On the other hand, the neo-orthodox reacted against certain liberal concepts such as the use of reason or natural theology.

Here we must pause to define some terms. Ever since Thomas Aquinas there has been a distinction between natural and revealed theology. Natural theology is man's philosophical study of religion. It is what man can learn about God, immortality, and such questions by the use of reason alone. It appeals to facts and theories that are available to any rational man. It is distinguished from revealed theology, which begins with the belief that God has given a special revelation of himself. Thus Aquinas believed that natural theology can prove that God exists, but it requires revealed theology to inform us that he exists as a Trinity. It may be summed up quickly by saying that natural theology represents man's search for God; revealed theology represents God's search for man. The liberal, with his emphasis upon reason and experience, emphasized natural theology. Neo-liberalism gave revealed theology a new hearing without abandoning natural theology. Neo-orthodoxy generally repudiates natural theology.

The term neo-orthodox never accurately described a school of thought. It was applied to men who had little in common except that they rejected both liberal and fundamentalist alternatives. In time it became apparent that some of the primary theological debates were between men who had been grouped as neo-orthodox. The next chapters will attempt to indicate some of the diversity within neo-orthodoxy.

SOREN KIERKEGAARD

The man who inspired many neo-orthodox tendencies was the strange Danish philosopher-theologian, Soren Kierkegaard (1813-1855). In the nineteenth century Kierkegaard was a voice crying in the wilderness of a complacent civilization. His cry went unheeded except for the self-satisfaction which newspaper editors got from plaguing him. But in the anxiety, loneliness, and despair of the twentieth century the words of Kierkegaard began to sound to many as true prophecies. His experience, which was unique in the nineteenth century, has become common in the twentieth. In many ways he has seemed more up-to-date than any philosopher that our own century has produced. He has inspired the philosophy known as existentialism, which has Christian, Jewish, agnostic, and atheistic exponents.

The facts of Kierkegaard's tragic life are well known and we will not recount them here. The interested reader can find several excellent summaries of Kierkegaard's thought. Here we shall look at a few of his basic ideas which inspired theology in our century.

Kierkegaard is an existentialist thinker, that is, he insists that true thought must begin with the fact of a concrete man in a concrete situation. Abstract truths about man might be true of all men in general, but they would describe no man in particular. Whereas Descartes starts his philosophy withdrawn from life, alone and engaged in pure reasoning, Kierkegaard begins with man as he actually exists in his daily relationship with God, the universe, and other men.

Kierkegaard revolted against abstract thought in philosophy and religion. In science or mathematics we can deal objectively with facts without ourselves being deeply concerned with them. But in philosophy and religion the aim is never to know dogmas or ideas but to live them. He protests against those philosophers who build magnificent houses of theory but who do not choose to dwell in them. The aim of true religious or philosophical thinking is to bring man to commit himself to a way of life. If thought does not help man to answer the question, "What ought I to do?" it is a betrayal of man.

We particularly need the existential method, thinks Kierkegaard, when we deal with God or man. In objective thought we think coldly and rationally of objects separate from ourselves. We are not vitally concerned with them in our whole being. They concern our mind or reason only. But it degrades both God and man to make them into objects of this nature. God can never be just an object of man's thought; he is the living challenge who forces man to make a decision. God is subject and not object when he comes into contact with man. Similarly, when we think of others or ourselves as objects, we dehumanize man. We must see man as a subject, the center of a willing, thinking, hoping, passionate process. Man is a self, not a thing.

With this goes an emphasis upon man as an individual. Kierkegaard foresaw what has become so demonic in our day: the tendency to submerge the individual into the mass, to make him simply another cog in the wheel of society. Man can cease to be truly human by allowing himself to be swallowed by the crowd. Existentialism fights to preserve man as the one who makes his own decisions in concrete situations. Kierkegaard deplored the fact that people in the Christian Churches were stereotyped into Church members instead of being free, independent individuals who were answerable to God.

Turning to his interpretation of Christianity, we find that Kierkegaard poses a new question. Both the fundamentalists and the liberals have been preoccupied with the content of religious faith. The fundamentalists believe that we have a set of divine truths which are proved by the authority of Scripture. Liberalism believes that in Christianity we find the highest expression of those truths which man knows dimly everywhere. Kierkegaard opposes both by asking, not what is the content of Christianity, but what does it mean to be a Christian? How does one become a Christian? Of course, the differences are relative, but it is interesting to recall Fosdick's charge that liberalism was overly concerned with the intellectual problems of Christianity.

The problem was made urgent for Kierkegaard because he felt that the members of the state Church in Denmark were not Christian; they were only nominal Christians. Being a nominal Christian actually prevented one from becoming a true Christian. Furthermore, for Kierkegaard this became the question of how one becomes truly human. Just as membership in the Church does not make a man truly Christian, so being born a man does not make one truly human. In essence, Kierkegaard answers that we are not saved; that is, we do not become Christian and human by coming to know something that we did not know before; rather we are saved by the transformation of our existence and life through divine grace. The gospel is not a new philosophy; it is the act of God which comes to solve the problem of man's despair. Kierkegaard is convinced that one does not become a Christian; he simply strives to become one. He may start on the path but he will not reach the goal.

Kierkegaard believed that one could only become a Christian by a leap of faith, a radical commitment of one's whole life. That is because man's reason comes up against a boundary beyond which it cannot penetrate. The reason which can prove things in science is incapable of using the same methods to understand God, for God can never be just an object whose existence can be proved or disproved. When God is known he appears paradoxical to our reason. The God that men claim to find in their philosophies is but an image of themselves. The real God can be found only in so far as he makes himself known as a living factor in life.

But the leap is not irrational even if reason cannot

prove its desirability. When man studies his true situation he is driven to despair, and in his despair he is ready to grasp the salvation that God offers to him. Man sees that he is bound by the finite world but he is pulled toward the infinite. His dreams exceed his grasp. He longs for the good life but fails to live it. So long as man eats, drinks, and is merry he may hide from himself the underlying anxiety and insecurity of life. But the minute he takes seriously the ethical life, he is brought to despair by his failure.

Doubt is never completely overcome; but in the leap of faith whereby he chooses to follow Christ, man has the moral certainty of his conviction. With Kierkegaard, modern theology finds a new understanding of religious certainty. Kierkegaard promises no certainty; he offers instead a leap which is always, in part, a leap in the dark and a gamble that there is a God. Faith means the betting of one's life upon the God in Jesus Christ.

Faith does not mean for Kierkegaard the believing of doctrines that cannot be proved; it means the giving or commitment of one's whole life. There is no halfway house; one either accepts or rejects Christ. Those Christians who try to hide in the Church as respectable persons are seeking a halfway house, but they are greater enemies of Christ than the atheist. He had particular scorn for preachers who made a good living out of preaching about the crucifixion of Christ. For Kierkegaard, to become a Christian one had to give his whole life to the dangerous and lonely task of following God. It was dangerous and lonely because it had always to be lived against the crowd and often against the Church. The Christian life is a life of suffering; there is no simple peace of mind in Christianity for Kierkegaard.

Kierkegaard's God is always transcendent. This is not a philosophical doctrine to be set against the liberal's doctrine of immanence. Instead, it means that man is separated from God by his sin and guilt. Man cannot lift himself to God; God must come to man. Even in the leap of faith to God, God must act. Although Kierkegaard repudiated predestination, he was aware that without the help of God we cannot find God.

This, in too brief an analysis, is something of what Kierkegaard has to say. His thinking has stirred modern theology. By analyzing man's despair, anxiety, and sin he threw doubt on the nineteenth century's optimism. His analysis of reason forced theologians to take a new look at how we can think about God. Can we speak about God in the same way that we speak about the physical world? We shall meet Kierkegaardian themes frequently in the following pages.

EMIL BRUNNER

What is called neo-orthodoxy was founded primarily by Karl Barth. For many years Barth's thought was not well known in America and a number of misunderstandings remained current until his *Church Dogmatics* was translated in the nineteen fifties. As a result, most Americans learned their first neo-orthodoxy from Emil Brunner who lectured in this country several times and whose basic works were translated earlier than Barth's.

Brunner was born in Switzerland in 1889. He studied at Zurich, Berlin, and Union Theological Seminary in New York. After an eight-year pastorate he joined the theological faculty at Zurich in 1924. In 1953 he left Zurich to teach in the Christian University of Japan. During this time his health suffered; however, after returning to Switzerland, he completed the final volume of his *Dogmatics* despite a stroke that made it impossible for him to write. He learned the art of composing his theology through a dictaphone. In 1966 Brunner died.

Brunner first became known to the English-speaking world as an exponent of "dialectical" or "crisis theology." The concept of dialectic has been known in philosophy since the time of Socrates. It describes the attempt to find truth by allowing opposite positions to come into debate. For dialectical theology God's revelation is related to man's knowledge in such a way that it is never the fulfillment of man's expectations about God. When God speaks to man there is a paradox. Theology is an incomplete and finite expression of the paradoxical relationship to God that can never be fully expressed in human terms.

This position was called "crisis theology" because it taught that a crisis occurs when God confronts man. In a medical history the crisis is the turning point at which the patient turns either toward death or new health. Similarly, for this theology, when God confronts man, man's total future hangs in the balance. He can say "no" to God and turn to death or he can say "yes" and become a new man.

As Brunner's theology developed he emphasized

"truth as encounter." In science and philosophy man thinks in terms of the subject (the man who thinks) and the object (about which the subject thinks). This leads to the distinction between objective and subjective thinking. Objective thinking is limited and tested by the object. The objective thinker lets the facts speak for themselves regardless of his personal preferences or wishes. Science and philosophy put a high evaluation upon objective thinking. On the other hand, subjective thinking takes on the connotation of thinking with one's feelings and ignoring the objective facts. Much of the history of philosophy has been a debate about the relative values of objective and subjective thinking and an analysis of how subjective elements affect our perception of the object.

To Brunner it is tragic that theology has allowed itself to be controlled by the dichotomy of subjective and objective thinking. When the Church thinks objectively it assumes that revelation consists of truths which God reveals to man through the Bible and the Church. Knowledge of God is thus objectively available. There have always been Christians who were disturbed by objectivism. They knew that the devil himself can quote Scripture or doctrine with accuracy. When such Christians have assumed that the only alternative to objectivity is subjectivity, they have revolted in the name of subjectivism. They have stressed the importance of man's inner experience, his "faith." They have called on men to look within themselves to find the living truth that cannot be objectively observed. But wherever subjectivism appears, each individual becomes his own ultimate authority and the

Church is split by mutually incompatible private revelations.

Brunner argues that objectivism and subjectivism are not the only alternatives. In the Bible and the Reformation we find an alternative which Brunner calls "truth as encounter." Here thinking is dialectical; it looks both to the Word of God in the Bible and to the Witness of the Holy Spirit within, both of which are experienced as a unity.

When we turn to the Bible we find that God always takes the initiative to make himself known to man. God does not reveal new information or doctrines; he reveals himself. In this way the subject-object relationship is overcome. God does not reveal himself as an object for thought but as a person who enters into personal relationship with man.

To develop his concept, Brunner uses the distinction between I-it and I-thou relationships which was inspired by Kierkegaard and popularized by the Jewish philosopher-theologian Martin Buber. I-it knowledge is objective knowledge of an object as a thing outside of ourselves. In I-it knowledge the knower is detached; he has no vital concern with the object. There is no communion between the known and the knower. The best example of I-it knowledge is the scientist who stands outside of his experiment controlling and manipulating it in detachment from it.

We may have a purely I-it knowledge of another person. We may observe him like any other object, we get information about him, we list his characteristics, and we put him into the appropriate category. We use and manipulate him for our purposes. But there is another way in which we can know a person—the way of I-thou. The other person ceases to be an "it" or a "something" and becomes a "thou" to us. He reveals not information about himself but his very self, and we give of ourselves in return. An I-thou relation has replaced the objective relationship in which we were as two things facing each other. There is now communion. No longer is one an onlooker who may be enlarged by more information. Instead, he is changed to the very core of his being because he knows and gives himself to the other.

This personal relation is the best analogy to our knowledge of God. It is a mistake to suppose that we can have an objective knowledge of God because this would imply that God comes into our power and is held, controlled, and manipulated by us. This, believes Brunner, is the mistake of Roman Catholicism and fundamentalism. Each believes that it has, in its system, infallible truths about God which it can use to judge others and to win salvation for itself. But God is truly known only in an I-thou relation. It is the essence of the I-thou relation that we never possess, control, or manipulate the other. In this experience we approach each other and commune in freedom, giving of ourselves freely. The same principle applies to the I-thou relation with God; we cannot possess or hold God in our creed, Bible, or Church. God remains free. Revelation does not give some knowledge about God; it is God giving himself. God must give himself because only God can reveal God.

This explains why natural theology or philosophy can never have an adequate knowledge of God. In philosophy we are thinking about God; God is an "it," an object whose existence or nonexistence can be debated. When a philosophy class discusses the proofs of God, it may have a most pleasant time; it may even learn something about the use of logic. But it can learn nothing about the God whom Christians worship, for the word "God" means something entirely different in the two spheres. This is proved, among other things, by the fact that no great difference in the lives of two men is noticeable, although one has accepted the proofs for this "God's" existence and the other has rejected them. But the God of Christian revelation cannot be so blithely discussed, accepted, or rejected. To know this God is to be shaken to the depth of one's being and to be remade.

Although Brunner disparages the role of natural theology, he broke with Karl Barth over this question in the thirties. Brunner was criticized by Barth because Brunner argued that the image of God is still to be found in sinful man and that God is revealed in nature. Taking a stand against the liberals, Brunner argues that man, so long as he is a sinner, can learn nothing about God because he is blinded by his sin. But against Barth he argues that if man were no longer in the image of God and if there were not a revelation of God in nature, man could not be held responsible for his sin.

When man's reason is freed by God's revelation, it can and should be used to show the reasonableness of the Christian faith, argues Brunner. Thus, in showing that the subject-object method of thinking is inappropriate to thinking about God, Brunner is using reason to demonstrate the reasonableness of Christian faith. Furthermore, the theologian ought to use reason to answer alternatives to the Christian faith. Reason cannot convert a man to Christianity (only the encounter with God in Christ can do that) but reason can prepare the ground for conversion and can remove intellectual obstacles.

In his doctrine of sin Brunner accepts the Augustinian analysis of original sin but repudiates Augustine's theory that it is inherited. The essence of sin, says Brunner, requires a free decision. Sin is the result of man's choice, not his heredity. Man is created by God to live in harmony with God, but instead he chooses to live a life centered around himself. He withdraws into his "I castle" and can only be brought out when God comes to him with love and, winning his confidence, overcomes man's anxiety and enables him to give himself away.

The Bible points to a particular time and place where, in Jesus Christ, God chose to make himself known. Christianity, therefore, remains a "scandal" to the modern mind which desires to find a God who may be known anywhere at any time by anyone who tries hard enough. Behind this modern desire there is a refusal to face the fact of man's sinful preoccupation with himself. We cannot logically deduce how the just God is going to behave toward sinners. It is only because God has actually appeared to reveal his forgiving nature that we are able to speak with assurance of God's forgiveness of sin. Because of man's sin, God can be known only through a mediator, Jesus Christ, who comes from God with the revelation that man could not find for himself.

Brunner is confident that there is no such thing as Christian faith apart from Christian conduct. His book *The Divine Imperative*, a volume of nearly 600 pages, is one of the classic treatments of Christian ethics to be written in this century. He spends the first part of that book in analyzing the theological basis for ethical living and then turns to the application of that analysis to specific spheres such as the state, the economic system, and the family.

Brunner starts with the recognition that every man has some concept of what he believes to be the good life. As a fact of history, he finds that morality has been closely connected with religion and that all religions have a concept of a law which comes from a divine will. Despite this, there has been, since the time of Socrates, an attempt to find a rational ethic which does not depend upon a revelation of God. This attempt may or may not be irreligious, but its religion must be one that is known by man's reason alone.

From the efforts of rationalists we get two basic systems—the naturalistic and the idealistic. The naturalistic systems treat man as a product of nature, an animal, and try to find in nature the clue to good living. Such ethics have to face a dilemma. Man is conscious of a "sense of ought" which often calls him to do what does not come naturally. Either the naturalist must deny the validity of such a consciousness or he must bring a non-naturalistic element into his system.

The idealists, most of whom are influenced by Kant,

try to build an ethic upon the basis of duty for duty's sake. Man is aware of the "categorical imperative," the sense of feeling that he ought to do something regardless of inclination or the profit to be gained by the act. But, asks Brunner, what can "Thou shalt" mean if it does not come from God? Who is the legislator that makes it right? Idealism forces us to split the personality so that we think in terms of a better self which legislates to our worse self. In Kant, his own Christian training shines through his thought and colors it continually where he believes that he is using reason alone. But in others this kind of ethic can lead to identifying one's inclination with one's duty.

In his book *Justice and the Social Order,* Brunner analyzes what happens to the concept of justice when it loses its basis in the will of God. The age of rationalism explained the sense of justice in terms of man's reason alone. In the nineteenth century the positivists, denying all supernaturalism, insisted that justice is a purely relative matter, varying from one place to another. They denied that there is any eternally valid concept of justice standing over human legislation. From this it followed inevitably, believes Brunner, that states should grow up which would cast aside all traditional concepts and proclaim that the only standard of justice is the will of the ruling power. In short, you get totalitarianism, in which the state can do no wrong because there is nothing higher than the law of the state by which it could be judged. Hence, if there is no "sacred, eternal, divine, absolute law," it is impossible to denounce any law or national act as unjust. We cannot attack the totalitarian state as a monster of injustice; we can only say, "It does not suit me; I do not like such things."

In Christianity Brunner finds the alternative to naturalistic positivism or subjective idealism. In the Bible goodness has its basis solely in the will of God. It is God who speaks the "Thou shalt." In the face of this command we can understand the full meaning of guilt, but we do so without despair for with the knowledge of guilt comes the assurance that it can be overcome by forgiveness.

In the light of this law we find that all men are sinners; all have fallen short of God's will. It is only through the mercy of God that we can be considered righteous. The worst sin is not, therefore, any of the obvious vices; it is the pride of the man who thinks he is good enough and who looks with scorn upon other men. This man is continually forced to water down the demands of the law in order that he might justify himself and appear more righteous in his own eyes.

In Christianity goodness does not arise from a sense of duty. Obedience is not the fruit of a sense of ought but the free act of love. The self-centered man is lifted out of himself by God's love, which has no conditional "I will love you if. . ." This is the meaning of Christian freedom: man no longer has to obey a law; he freely does that which he has come to want to do. God does not give commands to slaves; he gives instructions to sons.

When love has freed man from law, it creates a new relation between a man and his neighbor. Love replaces the abstract law between them. No longer is the other man a "case" to which the unbending rule must be applied; he can be loved for what he is, and treated upon the basis of his individual need.

Society is organized in certain "orders of creation," such as the state, the family, and the Church. These are God-given orders, for apart from them there can be no stable community life. But, although they are God-given, they become tainted with sin, and the Christian does not owe unquestioning loyalty to any of them.

The tragedy of original sin becomes most apparent when we find that our calling in these orders forces us to do that which is evil. For example, a Christian judge must enforce laws even when they are unjust. He knows that society must observe law in order to exist, and so, with a heavy heart, he must administer the unjust law. Nevertheless, he is not confined to his official role alone, and it may be possible to mitigate the sting of injustice in some personal relation with the man who has been wronged. Where a system of law is wrong, it is the Christian's duty to work for a better law; but he must not forget that any law which keeps order is the best until a better order can be achieved.

Because Brunner's thought seemed to be more open to natural theology than that of other neo-orthodox theologians he was more welcome to liberal theologians in America. Brunner's strong defense of America's anti-Communist stance in the cold war endeared him to many Americans. In his analysis of the I-thou relationship as a clue to thinking about God, Brunner made a permanent contribution to theology. In recent years, however, Brunner's influence has waned. Other theologians have moved to the center of the stage. Time alone will tell whether Brunner's work will be rediscovered at a later stage or whether his work will be seen as only a transitional stage in the development of twentieth-century theology.

6

Karl Barth

In 1919 the peaceful atmosphere of European theology was thrown into confusion by a commentary on
the Book of Romans written by an unknown parish
minister, Karl Barth. One writer says that Barth took
a letter written in first century Greek and made it a
special delivery to twentieth century man. Every modern theologian owes something to Barth, even if he
has only reacted against him. Today it is often said
that we live in a post-Barthian age. But, if so, this age
also bears the marks of Barth's contribution.

Barth was born in 1886 in Basle, Switzerland, and
studied under liberal theologians such as Harnack
and Hermann. In 1911 he began a ten-year pastorate
in the Swiss village of Safenvill where he wrote his
commentary on Romans. In 1921 he became a professor in Göttingen and in 1929 he went to teach at
Bonn. Barth watched the rise of Hitler with concern
and became one of the founders of the Confessional
Church which resisted the attempts of the "German
Christians" to unite Christianity and Nazism. He
helped to draft the famous Barmen Declaration
which, in the face of Hitler's totalitarianism, declared
that the Church's only *führer* was God. In 1935, having refused to take a loyalty oath to Nazism, he had to

flee from Germany. He accepted a chair of theology at Basle from which he retired in 1962.

Barth began as a liberal theologian hoping that the Kingdom of God could be built by the efforts of dedicated men. The First World War came as a shock to his optimism. As he watched the civilized nations plunge themselves into the orgy of destruction, he felt that man's situation was too desperate to be solved merely by changing the political and economic structures. For a time he was perplexed by the demands of his weekly sermon. People came to hear him each week but what could he say? Too often they went away disappointed because his sermon was not confronting the questions that troubled them the most.

Barth turned to the theologians but found that they had no help for a village preacher. They ignored the problems of preaching because theology had become university-centered rather than church-centered. Later, as a theologian, Barth remained convinced that the only excuse for the existence of a theologian is that he should be a servant and a critic of the preacher. When theologians ignore the task of the preacher, they end up mumbling about God and forgetting that they have a higher purpose than dishing out, in a slightly different form, the same ideas that already are popular in the modern world.

Finding no help in theology, Barth turned to the Bible where he found a "strange new world" that was more alive than the latest philosophy. He had no intention of becoming a theologian; he only hoped that, from the perspective of the Bible, he could add a "pinch of cinnamon" to flavor the theology of others.

But after his commentary on Romans appeared he was catapulted to the center of theological discussion. He likens himself to a man who was falling in the dark and reached out for support. To his surprise he found that he had caught a bell rope and the ringing of the bell had awakened the whole town.

Barth's theology is difficult to summarize because he has written more than any other theologian since Aquinas. His major work, *Church Dogmatics*, has reached over eight thousand pages and still is not complete. He is also difficult to summarize because his thought has undergone significant changes. He emphasizes that theology is a finite and human effort which needs to be kept in a spirit of constant reform and revision. Theology needs to be related to its own time. It is never enough merely to repeat what the great theologians of the past have said. They were great because they brought the Word of God to their age. Instead of repeating them, we must do for the present what they did for their times. Barth tells his students that they should read with the Bible in one hand and the newspaper in the other.

Since the world has changed during Barth's lifetime, it is not surprising that his theology has changed. There are, however, basic themes that run through his theology so that it has a fundamental consistency. Barth's whole theology has been based upon his conviction that for more than a century theology had pursued a false direction. It was trying to go from man to God. Schleiermacher taught that when men look into their selves they can find God. Ritschl led men to find God in their ethical concern. Others found God in man's mystical experiences or in man's reason. Barth says that all of these roads from man to God are dead-end streets. In the Bible man does not seek God, God seeks man. Throughout all of the changes in his theology, Barth's concentration upon God's search for man has not changed.

Barth distinguishes between religion and faith. Religion is man's search for God and it always results in man finding a god that he wants to find. This is not intended as a criticism of non-Christian religions only, because Christians also build religions and Barth's deepest criticisms of religion are directed at Christian religions. Jesus is the revelation that destroys religion. The early Christians were called atheists because they destroyed the man-made gods of their time. Therefore it would be a healthy sign if Christians were still suspected of atheism.

Because God is the living God, Barth warns against identifying the Word of God with any human form or institution. Not even the Bible can be identified with the Word of God. The error of fundamentalism, as he sees it, is that it takes the Bible as a "self-sufficient Paper-Pope." To Barth the words of the Bible and of the human Jesus are "tokens." One may read the Bible without hearing the Word of God. But the Word does come to us through these tokens. Some day, as we read a passage of Scripture, it may suddenly come alive and speak to us in the situation in which we find ourselves. The writers of Scripture wrote to tell of the revelation they received from God and, as we read, the same God who spoke to them may speak to us. Thus, says Barth, the Bible is a record of a past revelation and a promise of future revelation.

Revelation, for Barth, does not mean that we are

given some new information or theology that we could not have discovered for ourselves. God reveals not information but himself. The Word of God is always spoken to a particular man in a particular situation. When God calls, says Barth, he does not call station to station, he calls person to person.

In his early writing Barth emphasized that God is "Wholly Other." Critics have objected that if God is truly wholly other, then we cannot understand anything about him even if he reveals himself. But Barth never denied that there is an analogy between God and man whereby man can understand God. By calling God Wholly Other, Barth first wanted to say that God is a reality apart from us. He refused to use the word "God" to describe the "spirit of humanity" or the "value-producing aspects of the universe." Furthermore, he wanted to emphasize that we cannot come to know God by starting with man at his best and adding a few superlatives. God is not the culmination of all that is good in man. Even when man has done his best he is still an unworthy servant who must look to God for forgiveness.

Because Barth denies man's ability to learn of God through reason, it is often assumed that he is an irrationalist. Certainly, in his early works Barth could say some harsh things about reason, but actually his position is consistently rational. He distinguishes between a priori and a posteriori reasoning. A priori reasoning claims to know truths apart from experience. When Barth denies that man can know God through reason he denies that man has any a priori knowledge of God. If man did have a priori knowledge of God he would have a criterion by which he could judge God's revelation. A posteriori reasoning is that which we can undertake after we have experienced an event. Barth insists that all knowledge of God is a posteriori. We cannot know who God is until he reveals himself. We cannot know a priori that God is love; we only learn that after the life of Christ makes God's love manifest. However, after God does reveal himself, Barth insists that man must use his reason to understand what God has said.

Barth's experience under Nazism did much to reconfirm him in his emphasis that we can know God only through revelation. Many theologians argued that Barth's position was irrelevant because he had divorced revelation from man's history and culture. These theologians asserted that we must learn of God from history as well as from the Scriptures. When Hitler came to power most of them tried to accommodate Christianity to Nazism. For a century theologians had attempted to modernize the faith by accommodating it to the modern age. Now, in Germany, Hitler was the modern age and thus it seemed logical to accommodate Christianity to this latest form of modernity. We have seen that Barth would agree with his critics that theology must change with changing times. But there the agreement ends. Barth would learn from his age *how* to express the Christian faith but the modern age cannot reveal *what* we are to say. What we say is rooted in God's revelation and not in the present age. Those who had charged Barth with presenting a timeless revelation that was irrelevant to modern man had little to say about Nazism. Some of them joined the

German Christian Movement that tried to unite Nazism and Christianity. Others wavered between acceptance and mild criticism. Barth proved to be relevant to his situation precisely because he witnessed to a Word that stood in judgment on every age.

In his early writing Barth was deeply influenced by Kierkegaard. From Kierkegaard he accepted the view of the qualitative distinction between time and eternity. Much of what the early Barth said about the wholly other God was based on the concept that time and eternity, man and God, are utterly opposite. This means that it is an absolute paradox to say that Jesus is both God and man. In the late twenties Barth began writing his *Dogmatics* and completed one large volume. When critics pointed out that it was dependent upon existentialist philosophy, Barth began all over again. This was the most decisive turning point in his theological development. Henceforth he dedicated himself to building his theology on the Bible alone and, being freed from the concept of the absolute distance between God and man, he was able to take the Incarnation of Christ more seriously. Whereas his early theology put emphasis upon the Holy Spirit as the prime point where God meets man, he has shifted to make Christ the center of theology.

Barth now argues that it is a fallacy to see the Incarnation of God in Christ as a paradox. It seems a paradox because we assume that, apart from Christ, we know who and what both God and man are and we cannot see how our ideas of God and man can exist in the same person. But, says Barth, if we do not begin with a priori assumptions but rather find in Christ the revelation of both God and man, the paradox disappears. In Christ we find that God includes humanity within himself. Man can understand God's revelation because man is created in the image of God's own humanity.

Barth's point is illustrated by his discussion of God's omnipotence. To say that God is omnipotent is to say that he is all-powerful. So long as man thinks in an a priori way, he thinks of God's power by analogy with what he would like to be if he had unlimited power. Thus it seems absurd for God to become weak and to be born in a manger and to die upon a cross. But if we begin a posteriori in light of the revelation of God in Christ, we get a totally different picture of what God's omnipotence means. It means that God has the power to become weak and to walk the way of the cross. God proves that he, not the gods of men's imaginations, is truly powerful because, unlike man's gods, he dares to be weak and powerless. Instead of sitting upon a throne on high, as man would do if he were omnipotent, God comes to man in humility. Instead of demanding subservience, God comes as one who serves.

Christ is the revelation of the true God and also of the true man. Because Barth began his theological revolution in disillusionment with the liberal optimism about man, it is often thought that Barth substituted a pessimistic for an optimistic view of man. This is incorrect. At an early date Barth rebuked some of his own followers because they were putting too much emphasis upon man's sin and depravity. We cannot glorify God by disparaging man, he emphasized. It is true that if we look at man in history we see that he is a sinner. The pages of history disclose man's inhumanity to man. But when we look to Christ as the true man we see that sin is not a part of man's true nature.

Barth does believe that man, apart from God, inevitably falls into sin. But, in Christ, God reveals that he is not willing to let man exist in sin. Thus Barth insists that we should never mention sin unless we immediately go on to say that sin has been overcome, forgiven, and defeated in Christ. Jesus once said that with man certain things are impossible but that with God all things are possible (Matt. 19:26). This is the theme of Barth's doctrine of man. Because all things are possible with God, Barth puts great emphasis upon the new life which, by the power of God, man may live. G.C. Berkouwer named his book on Barth, *The Triumph of Grace in the Theology of Karl Barth*. It was a brilliant title because few theologians have written so vividly about God's triumph over sin or given such a firm promise of a new life for man.

The basis for Barth's optimism can be found in his doctrine of atonement. We have seen that, for Barth, God reveals his omnipotence by becoming weak. This means that, in Christ, God has gone into "the far country" where man lives as a prodigal. God is not content to dwell in heavenly isolation but wills to be with man. When the Christian ethic calls us to bear the burdens of others it is because God bears the burdens of others. When we are called to love our enemies, it is because God loves those who are his enemies. God reveals that he loves "the world" and not just the Jews, Christians, or good people. Because God loved and came into the world, his Church is called to serve the world.

In going into the far country, the Son became flesh. That is, he accepted the full nature of man with all of its temptations and problems. He stood where we stand. But Christ did not become just any flesh, he became Jewish flesh. For Barth the Jews hold a unique place in Christian theology. God, in his desire to win mankind, chose the Jews that he might work through them. The Old Testament is the story of how God remained faithful to the Jews even when they were not faithful to him. To them he gave his promises for all men and so, when the Son went into the far country, he became a Jew to fulfill the promises made to Abraham, Isaac, and Jacob.

While Hitler was slaughtering six million Jews, Barth turned with a new vision to Romans 9-11 where he found an understanding of the Jews that was opposed to most popular Christian views of them. The typical Christian view has been that in the Old Testament times the Jews were God's chosen people but, when they rejected Christ, they ceased to be the chosen people and were replaced by the Church. Some Christians have gone further and argued that the Jews are under a curse for having crucified Christ. Barth finds that all such views are repudiated by Paul.

From the beginning the Jews were chosen because of God's grace, not because of their own goodness. In the same way, Christians depend upon God's grace. If the disobedience of the Jews could result in their ceasing to be God's chosen people, then the Christian, who is also always disobedient, would have no reason to hope that God would keep his promises to him. Since God became Jewish flesh in Christ, the people of God have existed in a twofold form—the Synagogue and the Church. Paul sees that both have their place in God's purpose.

To Barth it seemed that Hitler had a demonic understanding of a truth most Christians had missed. Hitler knew that he had to exterminate the Jews because, as long as the Jews existed, they were a witness to the living God who stood in judgment over every dictator's claim to have ultimate authority. (Barth has said that the best proof of God's existence is the existence of the Jews.) Barth saw in Hitler's persecution of the Jews a declaration of war on God. Thus Barth rightly predicted that Hitler's persecution of the Jews would soon be followed by persecution of the Church.

Christ came as a Jew and identified himself with his people and their sin. In assuming flesh Christ was open to the same temptations as man, but he did not commit sin, thus revealing that sin is not of man's essence. Christ's life thus becomes a judgment of our lives. When we see true manhood in Christ we see that our self-centered lives are a distortion of our true nature. In Christ we see that our sin is that we have wanted to judge ourselves. Adam and Eve fell because they wanted to know good and evil as God knows it. To know good and evil as God knows it is to be the one who creates the distinction between what is good and evil. Each nation, class, and individual sets its own standards and mores and finds itself good. But when Christ came he revealed that we are under the judgment of God, not of ourselves.

If all that Christ did was to pass judgment upon us we would be more hopeless than before. But Christ also reveals that God is free to decide how his judgment shall fall and it falls upon himself in Christ rather than upon man. And, insofar as God passes judgment upon himself, he frees us from the need to judge ourselves. This is freedom because when man sets himself up as his own judge, he becomes vulnerable to the judgment of his neighbors. He is haunted by the need to have others think well of him. Sinful man is a strange mixture. At one moment he declares his own virtue with unseemly self-righteousness but at the next moment he looks around anxiously to see if others share his good opinion of himself. What a freedom is portrayed when Paul can say, "with me it is a very small thing that I should be judged by you or by any human court. I do not even judge myself . . . It is the Lord who judges me" (I Cor. 4:3-4). The Christian can speak this way because, when he is judged by Christ, he is judged by the one who speaks a word of forgiveness and promises a new life. God did not look lightly upon the sinful condition of the world, but neither did he sit aloofly and say, "Let the world go to Hell." He took the costly journey into the far country to become one of his own fallen creatures and to free them from judgment, separation from God, and the nothingness of death.

Since Christ we have no future as sinners. The ground has been cut from under us. In a sermon, Barth refers to a group of Japanese soldiers on a remote Pacific island who, fourteen years after the Second World War ended, were still shooting at anyone they saw because they had not heard that the war was over. Strange people, comments Barth, fighting a war that has been over for fourteen years! But not so strange as we are when we continue to live in sin two thousand years after Christ brought sin to an end.

Barth does not accept either Anselm's concept that Christ's death was a satisfaction of God's wrath or the idea that Christ was punished in our place. Such views are unbiblical because they imply that something happened to change God's mind about man. The whole point of Christ's Incarnation is that God would not forsake man; God's love would not allow sin to remain because man, by his sin, was destroying himself. God opened a new way for man to find peace. Christ, through his perfect repentance, did what man needed to do. He placed himself under the judgment so that man would be freed from judgment.

How can we claim today that we are those for whom Christ acted? Granted that the Son came into the far country and was the judge who was judged in our place—what does that have to do with us in the twentieth century? The only answer seems to be the ambiguous one that Christ's actions can speak to us because we hear about them from the Bible and preaching. But can such a word of release be meaningful when we hear about it at secondhand? Barth notes that contemporary theology has become concerned with the problem of how faith is related to history. But can history, with its doubts and ambiguities, really help at all?

Barth says that we can answer such questions only when we look to the Resurrection of Christ. For the first disciples, Christ's Resurrection was God's verdict about Christ. In raising Christ, God revealed that he had accepted Christ's repentance on their behalf. To be dead is to be nothing. To raise Christ from the dead required the same power by which God created the world out of nothing. By raising Christ, God promised his creation that he would not abandon it. He revealed that Christ is always with man; that he who went into the far country to be with his people is still with them.

Atonement is not a business transaction between God and Christ that could have been carried out as well on Mars as on earth. It means that a living Lord meets his people here and now. God has eternally within himself the Son who went into the far country, shared our lot, accepted our judgment, and died and rose again. The bridge between our time and the first century is not the dubious findings of historians; it is the living Lord Jesus. The Cross and the Resurrection called the Church into being. The Church member is a man who knows that the human condition is changed. The Church must be missionary; it must tell others; it must tell the soldiers still hiding behind the trees that the war is over. It is not the Church's telling that changes the situation: the situation of every man born into the world has been changed by the death and Resurrection of Christ. The peace treaty has been signed.

But, the skeptic asks, what is changed? Does not the world continue to have wars and rumors of wars? Do not men still suffer injustice? The New Testament, Barth reminds us, knew all of this as well as we do. The answer was not, as some suppose, that Christ was going to return soon to set up the perfect Kingdom. The men of the New Testament were not joyful because they expected that Christ was soon to return on the clouds of heaven. On the contrary, they looked for Christ's second coming because the presence of Christ with them was already so gloriously real. After the forty days of Christ's Resurrection appearances, they continued to know the presence of Christ through the mediation of the Holy Spirit. Men often ask what is new in Christianity. Neither its ethics nor its theology is unique. For Barth, the answer is that the uniqueness of Christianity is Christ himself. To be a Christian is to be a new man through knowing the reality of the crucified and risen Savior. The basis for all missionary work and preaching of the gospel is Jesus Christ.

The Resurrection of Christ, known as a reality through the Holy Spirit today, is the passing of God's verdict. If Christ had not risen, we could not tell men that their situation had changed. At best we could tell them that it might be changed if they had the power to make themselves like Jesus, but this would be bad news indeed, for who can do that? God's verdict tells us that what we could not do for ourselves, God has done for us. We are judged and forgiven; we are renewed through the power of the Holy Spirit. Barth's optimism about what God can do to make us new men is based on this new situation which God has brought into being.

When the Son went into the far country, he went in obedience to the Father. Similarly, the Christian is called to obedience, and Barth always has been concerned with the question of ethics—how is the Christian to live his obedience to God? Barth is sure that the Christian must serve God with his total life. He must be concerned with social and political affairs as well as with individual problems. One reason that Barth repudiated the liberal theology in which he had been trained was the behavior of his teachers during the First World War. He was appalled to find teachers whom he had admired giving unqualified blessing to the German cause. To Barth this demonstrated that these men, in their concern to relate themselves to the modern world, had lost the sense of God's judgment over the world.

Barth repudiates ethics which are bound by rules and regulations. Throughout the Bible God commands men in specific terms directed to their unique time and place. In Christ we find the pattern for our obedience and we must be disciples of Christ in each particular situation with its uniqueness and needs. In one sense this seems to leave the Christian without guidance because he cannot run his life by laws that are never to be broken. But, on the other hand, Christ is a concrete individual and loyalty to his spirit does not leave the Christian without concrete guidance for his behavior.

Why should we obey God? Non-Christians often assume that the Christian obeys God because God is an all-powerful cosmic policeman. Barth rejects this view. It would be utterly degrading for man to obey God just because God has the power to crush him if he does not. And it is no better to say that by obeying God man fulfills his own true nature. This is true but it still leaves obedience on a purely selfish plane. For Barth the only legitimate reason for obeying God is as a response to God for giving himself to us in love. In Christian obedience we are truly free. To do the will of one who loves us and whom we love in return is always a joy. The Christian does not obey out of fear or weakness; he obeys out of joy and strength. The man who obeys without joy is disobedient in the deepest sense. He is like the man in Jesus' parable who comes dutifully to the banquet because he is invited but fails to wear a wedding garment to express his joy.

The Christian must not be surprised to find those who do not claim to be Christian acting in the spirit of Christ. Often they put the Christian to shame. When this happens the Christian must not try to rationalize that their behavior is somehow not really good at all. On the contrary, this illustrates Barth's point that, in fact, the situation of all men has been changed by Christ. As a result, the Christian ought to thank God to see the spirit of Christ at work in one who does not confess Christ.

Christian discipleship calls us into a new relationship to things in the world—the family, the use of force, money, and the like. Each of these can become an idol. The danger of becoming too attached to things of the world, however, is no excuse for the Christian to reject them. This would be wrong because, in the first place, it would imply a lack of faith in God's power to keep man from sin if he is exposed to the things of the world. In the second place, it would be wrong because the Christian is not called to save his own soul. What he is called to do is to serve the world and he cannot do that if he shuns it.

The Christian will use the things of the world in a way that will be different from the world and which will displease the world. But the Christian must not seek to antagonize the world: when Daniel was in the lion's den he did not pull the lion's tail. Furthermore, the Christian is not called to fight against the world for it has enough trouble without the Christian adding to it. The Christian who is faithful to his Lord will, like his Lord, face the persecution and displeasure of the world. The Christian must expect that, in the terms of the title of one of Barth's books, he will have to swim *Against the Stream.*

Christian discipleship calls one to serve the State. It would be hypocritical to pray that the State be just if one did not work to make it just. Furthermore, as Barth learned under Nazism, the Christian may have to oppose the State. Even so, the Christian is acting for the State and not against it. He is objecting to its failure to be a true State. The State, as an institution, is given by God's grace to bless man. It is not to be worshipped; its power is limited by God's will. Although democracy cannot be identified with Christian faith and although men can be Christian under any form of government, Barth believes that Christians ought normally to work toward some form of democracy as the most adequate form of the State to serve man.

In the postwar world Barth has continued to express political ideas that go against the stream. In 1948, Brunner wrote an open letter to Barth criticizing him

for not opposing Communism as he had opposed
Nazism. Barth replied that the Church, in its obedience to Christ, must speak to concrete situations and
not in terms of general principles. The action of yesterday must not be repeated like a worn-out record;
the Church must seek God's will for today. Barth saw
the situation in 1948 quite differently from that of
1933. In 1933, Hitler was a real temptation to the
Western world. Praise for him was heard on all sides;
even Winston Churchill made some favorable comments. A number of influential Germans had organized the German Christian Movement to harmonize
Christianity with Nazism and had successfully infiltrated the Church. In 1948, Barth found the situation
quite different. Wherever he had travelled in the
Western world he found, with the exception of a piti-
ful little group of Communists, that everyone was
opposed to Communism. Any man was free to stand
up and oppose Communism and did. Why should the
Church feel called to say what every citizen could read
in his newspapers? Was not the real problem in the
West that it was inclined to give uncritical blessing to
its own way of life? Was not the Church in danger of
making anti-Communism into an absolute principle?

Karl Barth has left a rich heritage to theology. For
many years to come his *Dogmatics* will inspire new
theological research. He has won enthusiastic acclaim
from Roman Catholic theologians and his work has
done much to inspire the contemporary ecumenical
discussions between Protestants and Catholics. His
consistent attempt to build a theology around the act
of God in Christ and his joyous expression of Chris-

tian faith will win followers for many years. Perhaps those who claim that theology has entered into a post-Barthian period will prove to have been premature. On this continent Barth has been rather consistently misunderstood. (This misunderstanding was shared by the first edition of this book.) Future history may conclude that on this continent, at least, theology in the sixties was still pre-Barthian.

7

American Neo-Orthodoxy:
Reinhold Niebuhr

Reinhold Niebuhr was a professor of Christian ethics at Union Theological Seminary, New York, from 1928 to 1960. He was primarily interested in applying Christianity to political and social affairs. No other theologian has made such a deep impression upon the social sciences. In his later life Niebuhr sometimes has said that he was never a theologian but this cannot be taken seriously. For at least two decades his thought was the most important influence on theology in American seminaries. He, more than any other individual, is responsible for bringing neo-orthodox tendencies to America.

While he was a professor at Union Theological Seminary, Niebuhr was prominent in an incredible number of activities. He was a leader in the ecumenical movement of Protestantism. He ran several times for public office on the Socialist ticket and later was active in the top echelons of the New York Liberal party. Because he was one of the first political liberals to see the true nature and danger of Communism, he became one of the founding fathers of Americans for Democratic Action. There are few Christians who have given so much time and support to the Zionist cause.

Somehow he found time to write a host of books, edit two religious journals, and serve as a member of the editorial staffs of secular magazines. His articles have appeared in a countless number of secular and religious journals.

If we are to understand Neibuhr's theology, we must realize that it is not something which was thought up in the quiet of an academic environment. It grew out of his turblent life and his efforts to apply Christianity to the social, economic, and political spheres. Niebuhr's thinking always begins with the human, the material, and the social. He did not turn to orthodoxy because it was orthodox or because it came with some kind of dogmatic authority. He accepted it because he found in it the most adequate answer to the problems of social living.

Neibuhr graduated from a seminary in 1915 filled with the convictions of liberal theology. He believed in the goodness of God and man, in the desirability of applying the Sermon on the Mount to the whole of life, and in the optimistic hope that the Kingdom of God could be built upon earth in the relatively near future. Had he gone to a suburban middle-class church he might never have become a great theologian. He went, however, to a small working-class church in Detroit, where he saw at firsthand the problems of the worker, the tactics used to suppress union organization, and the tragic cost in human values that America was paying for its rapid industrialization. He began to doubt that the problems of the time could be solved as simply as his theology had led him to believe.

As time passed, the hard facts of life forced Niebuhr to realize that Christian orthodoxy was more realistic and intellectually respectable than liberal theology. In fact, Niebuhr desires that we should see his theology as simply a rediscovery of the lost wisdom of Christian orthodoxy. This does not mean that he turned to fundamentalism. His use of the term "myth" makes this clear.

The relation of man to God, the finite to the infinite, cannot, says Niebuhr, be expressed in purely rational or logical terms. It can only be expressed in myths such as the Genesis story of the creation and the fall. In religion, he believes, we are dealing with the mystery and depth of life which elude our efforts to catch them in neat rational descriptions. Niebuhr compares theology to a painter who, working upon a flat surface, tries to create the illusion of another dimension, depth. This is a deception, but a deception that describes a truth about reality. Similarly, the theologian must describe God and his ways in the thought forms of our space-time world. But God transcends the world so that none of the things we say can be adequate. On the other hand, God does not simply transcend the world; he is also immanent and active within it, so theology can say something about him. Since our earth-born logic can speak, but not adequately, about God, it must, like the painter, use symbols that point to another dimension of reality. Theology is the attempt to express the dimensions of depth in life. Niebuhr applies the term "myth" to this form of thinking. The term is perhaps unfortunate, as "myth" implies a fairy tale to most people. But by myth Niebuhr means that which, although it deceives, none the less points to a truth that cannot be adequately expressed in any other form. It is deceitful and yet true, just as is the deception of depth which is attained by the artist.

Fundamentalism takes the myths literally and thus enters into conflict with science over evolution. But such an interpretation is not only absurd science, it is also false religion. It oversimplifies the relation of God to the world. Liberalism saw in these myths only simple folk tales and pre-scientific speculation. Niebuhr, however, insists that we must take such myths seriously, but not literally. So interpreted they reveal true insights into the God-man relationship. For example, the story of Adam and Eve does not describe the first man and woman historically, but it is a mythical statement of the situation of every man and woman.

Niebuhr finds in the history of Christianity two attitudes toward reason. One has made Christianity completely irrational, over and above reason. It can neither be proved nor disproved by reason; any natural theology must be idolatry and any attempt to prove revelation is presumptuous. Niebuhr feels that this is dangerous because it destroys the meaning of the Gospel. If revelation has nothing to do with what we know by reason, how can we understand it? Furthermore, this way of thought lacks any standard by which we distinguish true from false revelation.

Side by side with the anti-rationalist Christian there has always been the rationalist Christian, says Niebuhr, from Origen and Aquinas to modern liberalism. This school has believed it impossible for reason and faith to contradict each other. Faith must be rational. The mistake of this school, believes Niebuhr, is that it prematurely grasps some principle of rationality to which all life must conform. It interprets all reality in terms of nature or mind, or in terms of nature and supernature. It knows clearly where reason ends and faith beings. In short, it pretends to know too much. As he puts it, it claims to know "the geography of heaven and hell, and the furniture of one and the temperature of the other." But life comes to us full of mystery and contradictions. We sense that there must be some meaning to the whole, some system, but if we try to find that meaning and system too quickly we fail to do justice to all of the facts. Niebuhr feels that most rational systems are too afraid to admit the paradoxes and contradictions of existence, and consequently they force life into their theories. They deny or ignore aspects of reality in order that they may keep their system coherent and rational. This is particularly true when they try to fit man into their systems, for man remains a paradoxical and contradictory creature. Any simply rational explanation of him must be an oversimplification.

Niebuhr lays a new basis for a rational defense of Christianity. In the first place, he insists that we must make a radical distinction between the natural world and the world of human history. The justification for this lies in the unique character of human freedom. Events do not happen in the life of man with the same necessity that rules nature. The social sciences cannot, in the very nature of things, predict events with the accuracy that we find in the physical sciences.

The events of history come to the believer as given; they cannot be anticipated by some rational theory. Among the events of history are those that reveal God. We find an analogy for revelation in our relations with other persons. We have evidence that there is in the other person a depth of reality that is more than just a physical organism. We have evidence that we are dealing with a "thou," not just a thing. We cannot know the other "thou" if we simply observe his behavior, because his real essence remains hidden. This other person can only be understood when he speaks to us and reveals something of the underlying depth of his being. The word which he speaks is at once a verification of the fact that we are dealing with a different dimension than that of physical existence alone, and it is a revelation of the precise character of the person with whom we are dealing. The same is true of God. We have intimations that this world points beyond itself, that it is not self-explanatory, that there is a depth of reality which does not meet the eye. But we cannot know this other dimension of reality unless it speaks and reveals itself to us. Christianity is based on the faith that God has spoken in the events of the Bible and particularly in the life of Jesus.

This faith in the revelation of God cannot be proved. To take Niebuhr's own illustration a step further, we may point out that neither can we prove that the character which another person reveals to us in his words is truth. In all love and friendship we accept the other's words in trust and faith. Similarly, we must accept the revelation of God with love, trust, and faith. But this does not leave us helpless. Niebuhr believes that the insights of revelation can be applied, by reason, to explain and understand the contradictory aspects of reality. Reason cannot of itself prove the truth of revelation, but, given the revelation, reason can show that it gives a more adequate picture of reality than any alternative. Niebuhr thus argues for the acceptance of revelation because he believes that the hypothesis of biblical revelation is the most adequate to explain and redeem human life.

Niebuhr demonstrates this by a twofold method. On the one hand, he attacks alternative hypotheses, such as humanism, to show that they fail to do justice to the whole of life; they explain too much away. On the other hand, he interprets the Christian hypothesis to show that it does do justice to the whole of life. The failure of modern philosophies to interpret or comprehend the disturbing facts of the twentieth century has made Christianity relevant. The failure of modern philosophies does not prove Christianity true; we must still walk by faith, but their failure does make it thoroughly reasonable to try Christian faith.

Niebuhr's most characteristic concept is that of original sin. This does not mean that man inherits Adam's guilt; it means that man falls naturally and inevitably into the sin of claiming for himself and his interests more than their objective importance would warrant.

Sin arises from the fact that man is a finite creature, an animal, who is capable of spirituality. That is, he is capable of thought, hopes, dreams, morality, and he is able, so to speak, to stand outside himself and to judge himself. The finite part of man threatens his spiritual nature. The meaning of life is threatened by man's dependence, animal nature, and inevitable death. Man longs for perfect knowledge, perfect freedom, perfect behavior, and perfect justice, but what he attains is always less than these. Because man is spiritual he needs to have a meaning for life, a reason for living. Because he is finite, every meaning that he finds is threatened. This dual nature of man results in anxiety. To overcome his anxiety man tries to grasp some ledge of security which will be safe from the vicissitudes of life. Man may sink into the sensuality of the animal and cease to strive for ideals, but more commonly he asserts himself, in pride, at the expense of others. Man refuses to recognize his limitations, and claims for himself that which belongs to God alone. Man's sin thus arises from the same source as his creativity and nobility. It does not detract from man's dignity to recognize that he is essentially a sinner, for sin is only possible in a creature who, in part, transcends a purely animal existence.

Pride manifests itself in three forms, each of which is an abortive attempt to find security and meaning for life in spite of its anxious insecurities. First, there is the pride of power. Power exalts a man and makes him feel more secure. It enables him to think that he is above the insecurities that plague the common run of mankind. The lust for power leads man to misuse his power over his fellow man through totalitarianism, racial discrimination, imperialism, and so on. Second, there is the pride of knowledge. Man claims to have the whole truth and nothing but the truth. Because any realistic admission of the relativities of his knowledge would threaten the meaning of life, he defends, often fanatically, his system of truth. He covers his anxiety by pretentious claims to a knowledge that he would like to have but never really has. Third, there is moral pride. This is classically portrayed by the Pharisee who uses his goodness and religion as a means to exalt himself over his fellow man. He thanks God he is not as others. This expresses itself in religious intolerance, persecution, and lack of sympathy for "sinners" on the part of the "good" people.

Normally, in the modern world, man expresses his pride by identifying himself with social groups such as nations, classes, churches, or races. He finds his security by identifying himself with the power, knowledge, or goodness of his group. This is one reason why religion is not necessarily good. Religion is simply the final battleground between God and man's pride. Religion may lead a man toward true humility or it may lead him to thank God that he has seen the light while lesser breeds without the law still move in darkness.

The chief problem of modern man, in Niebuhr's eyes, is his "easy conscience." Pride leads him to claim for himself a perfection that is not his. This self-righteousness blinds him to the justice and truth of those who oppose him. Man rationalizes his actions to make them appear to others and to himself as more just, ethical, and ideal than they really are. Consequently, the worst evils do not arise from pure selfishness; they arise from self-interest cloaking itself in high ideals. Even man's good actions are nullified by pride.

A Negro student once told me that she would not attend meetings of the Race Relations Society because she could not bear being used by its members to prove that they were more righteous in their racial attitudes than others. A member of any minority group will tell you that he prefers the bigots who hate him to the persons who go out of their way to round him up so that they may demonstrate their superior goodness. This illustrates Niebuhr's point that good actions lose their goodness when performed with pride. He finds copious illustration for his analysis in international relations, where the absolute self-righteousness of a nation makes impossible harmonious relations with other equally self-righteous nations.

The cure for man's sin lies in the Christian doctrine of salvation by grace. Man's sin does not lie in his animal nature or in his bodily desires. It arises from man's attempts to escape anxiety. As long as man believes that he is capable of conquering his anxieties and building his own security, he will be again tripped into pride. He must face realistically his insecurities and realize that they can only be overcome by God. Man's anxiety leads to sin when faith in God does not overcome anxiety. The Reformers were right: the basic sin is not any deed that man performs, but the separation from God which precedes the deed. By faith in God man can overcome his anxieties. This will protect against pride for two reasons. First, man realizes that it is God and not himself upon whom his security rests. Second, man, realizing his imperfection, knows that his relationship with God rests upon God's forgiveness and not upon his own righteousness. He can no longer scorn his "sinful" brethren, for he knows that he is as sinful as they are. Traditionally Protestants have argued that a man could not go to heaven unless he were saved by grace. Niebuhr argues that we cannot solve the major problems of social living without such salvation.

Niebuhr does not believe that even the Christian finds perfect security or freedom from pride. Pride ever waits to catch the Christian in the worst form of sin—the pride of being good. The Christian, however, has found the means whereby his pride may be humbled and to which he can return in repentance.

In the light of this, Niebuhr is critical both of secularists and of theologians who mutually condemn each other and claim that their believers are more righteous than the others. It is as silly for Christians to feel themselves morally superior by reason of their faith as it is for the secularists to regard themselves as superior for their lack of faith. Christians have some sorry blots upon their record, and many truths have come into history through secularism. The Church must learn the truth that secularism has to teach; it must admit that many of the values of our modern culture are due to secular contributions. The Christian believes that his religion contains a more ultimate truth than the philosophy of the secularist, but he cannot claim that because of this he is always more righteous and wise or that he ought to be more powerful. The major heresy for the Church, be it Catholic or Protestant, is for it to identify itself with God, to suppose that opposition to its way is opposition to God's ways. When the Church is guilty of such pretensions, it needs to be, and usually is, attacked by a secular force. The secular voice becomes a judgment of God upon a Church that has forgotten its true nature.

It is widely known that Niebuhr has spent most of his active life in battling for a more Christian social order. Yet many people insist that there is no basis in his theology for such action. His theology should, we are told, drive a man to despair and inaction. This misunderstanding is partly due to a failure to read Niebuhr with care, and partly due, as D. R. Davies suggests, to the failure of many in our day to understand the depths of life.

Niebuhr told in his classes a story which no doubt had considerable effect upon his thought and which illustrates his position. In his Detroit pastorate, while he still held a liberal theology, he was teaching a Sunday-school class about the Sermon on the Mount. Having expounded eloquently upon turning the other cheek, he was challenged by one of the boys in the class. This boy made a living for his widowed mother and family by selling papers. Each day, he said, there was a fight among the newsboys to see which one would get the best corner upon which to sell papers. Was he, as a Christian, to turn the other cheek, allow another boy to take his corner, and thus reduce the support that he could give to his family? Niebuhr found that his theology had no answer.

This story illustrates Niebuhr's belief that society never faces us with simple moral alternatives. The tragedy of social life is that one must choose the lesser of two evils rather than an abstract absolute good.

The man who insists upon following literally a system of moral absolutes will find that he is making an ineffectual attack upon social evils. Because he fails to see the ambiguity of his actions, he will fall into self-righteousness. We must recognize the tragic necessity of doing the best we can in the circumstances even if it is not an undiluted good.

This concept was first developed in the book with the suggestive title *Moral Man and Immoral Society*. In view of Niebuhr's doctrine of sin, it is clear that he did not think that individuals are moral. But he did insist that individual acts can be conducted on a higher moral level than social acts. Social situations are always an ambiguous mixture of good and evil, altruism and egoism. When a man attaches himself to a social group he does so with mixed motives. He is altruistic in his willingness to sacrifice himself and even die for his society. But egoism lurks in the background; it is "my country" for which he is ready to die. The original sin of pride can express itself through a society more naturally than through an individual. I can claim for my nation, my race, or my political party that which would be ridiculous if claimed for myself.

Because of the nature of society, reforms are never made simply because of a moral appeal. Capitalists did not reform the abuses of the capitalist system because preachers told them to love their neighbors. They reformed, grudgingly, when labor unions gained the power to force concessions. There is always a latent power struggle between nations and between societies within a nation. Justice is not gained by moral appeal but by establishing a tolerable harmony between the conflicting claims of groups.

Herein, insists Niebuhr, lies the Christian basis for democracy. Many theories of democracy are based upon the faith that man is rational and good and so should rule himself. This is an illusion. If man did not have a capacity for justice, democracy would be impossible. But it is man's sinfulness which makes democracy necessary. Democracy is necessary because no man is good enough to be allowed unchecked power over others; the original sin of pride means that man will misuse his power to exploit others if there is no control over him. Niebuhr believes that this was recognized by the writers of the American Constitution when they created the system of checks and balances to protect the people from too much power in any person's hands.

Niebuhr adopted from Barth the interpretation of the Christian ethic as an "impossible possibility." Jesus taught a perfect, and therefore an impossible, ethic, making no concessions to the weakness of man or to the relativities of the social situation. He demanded the absolute: "Resist not evil," "Be ye perfect." Jesus did not teach rules or laws for conduct; he taught an absolute principle—love. The ethic of Jesus is not, as the liberals thought, another expression of the prudential rules of conduct which the common sense of many ages has formed. On the contrary, Jesus teaches a love so perfect, so self-forgetting, that no man can attain it in the life of the world. But it is not an irrelevant ethic. While there is no situation in which the love-ethic can be applied perfectly, there is no situation in which we cannot come closer to fulfillment of the ideal than we have yet done. It stands in judgment over every situation and calls the Christian to lift up his eyes to a still higher goal.

Niebuhr's concept opposes two extremes. Against the general optimism of American life he has insisted upon the impossibilities of the ethic. Those who fail to see the perfection of Jesus' ethic usually end in complacently accepting as "Christian" a life which is nothing more than dull respectability. But against the despair of much European thought Niebuhr points to the possibilities. In every situation there are still untried opportunities to apply the spirit of love.

Niebuhr believes that it is impossible to identify Christianity with any social achievement. The Christian must be an eternal revolutionary. The kingdoms which we build are not the Kingdom for which we pray. Every social reform is ambiguous. It appears more just to those who profit from it than it does to those who do not. Furthermore, any advance made remains under the peril of later corruption and loss. One reformer can usually see the defects in another man's plans for reform, but the Christian, says Niebuhr, is the man who can see the defects in his own plan.

To Niebuhr, the great mistake of liberalism has been its belief that man is essentially good. Believing that man has sufficient resources in himself to obey the teaching of Jesus, it follows the Kantian principle, "If I ought, I can." Therefore, liberals have believed that the defects of society can be removed by changing the social system and by education. These theories founder on the rock of man's sin. Sin does not result from the imperfections of society; it causes them. When the old exploiters are removed, new exploiters appear.

This gives rise to a dilemma. If man faces realistically the limited possibilities of his achievements, how can he work for a better society? It is obvious that most reforms in the past have been brought in by men who were moved by the dream of a far more perfect society than anything that they achieved. Would they have worked with the necessary energy to create the limited reforms if they had not been filled with the illusions? Are illusions necessary to social progress? Niebuhr thinks not. In fact, they are a major cause for the perversion of reform. By self-righteously claiming too much, the reformer fails to guard against the latent evils within his system.

For Niebuhr the answer to the dilemma lies in taking seriously, but not literally, the apocalyptic teaching of the Bible. The apocalyptic teaching of the end of the world and the Second Coming of Christ has been perverted by those who continually forecast the imminent end of the world. But the depth of meaning in them must be kept. The Christian hope for history looks beyond history. God's resources for fulfilling his will are not limited by this world or this life. It is a grave mistake, however, to make Christianity simply an otherworldly religion. Apocalypse teaches that history is fulfilled, not denied. Hence the course of man's history, his victories over evil, have an ultimate importance in the final fulfillment beyond history.

The Christian can work for reform and progress

without being filled with illusions. Because he does not expect the Kingdom of God, or the perfect social order, upon this earth, he is not led into the despair into which the secular reformer often falls when the full difficulties of the task come to view. On the other hand, believing that anything which he can do will have significance in the ultimate fulfillment of history, the Christian is driven to action and does what he can even if there is no apparent hope of success.

Niebuhr is often looked upon as a prophet of gloom. It is true that against the background of American optimism he often has spoken sobering words that sounded pessimistic by contrast. But Niebuhr might well reply, as Dean Inge said in answer to those who had called him the "Gloomy Dean," "Things have turned out a lot worse than I prophesied." Niebuhr saw early in his career that both excessive optimism and despair are enemies of the Gospel and he has tried to steer a realistic course between them. In the fifties he pointed out that the prophets of doom had been proved wrong so far. They had forecast that if we followed certain policies there would be atomic war. But we followed the policies and war did not come. This illustrates for Niebuhr the fact that society is not run by iron laws of necessity. There is a freedom of choice involved, and we can never be certain about what is going to happen in history because man may use his freedom to do what was not foreseen. In this freedom lies the antidote both to despair and to excessive optimism. Because man has a certain freedom, although not absolute freedom, he may ruin a good society. Consequently, we cannot reasonably hope for an enduring Utopia. On the other hand, man can also use his freedom to improve any situation in which he finds himself. That is why we should never sit quietly in the midst of an evil situation; it can always be improved.

Because of his interpretation of the relationship between Christianity and social life, Niebuhr finds that the Christian may be called to several types of vocation. We need some Christian perfectionists who, like the pacifist, will refuse to compromise with the world and will live by absolute standards. Niebuhr feels that such a person is always partly deluded, for he is not as free from sin as he thinks. He depends upon the evils of society in a host of subtle ways. For example, he cannot buy food without paying taxes which support the war effort or other evil that he opposes. Despite this, the perfectionist forces other Christians to remember the full implications of Jesus' teaching and to realize that they are compromising with evil. He ought to move them to a sense of repentance.

Another Christian may be called to be a prophet who will hold the absolute demands of Christ before society and who will condemn the compromises that society must make. His function is to awaken the conscience of men and to force them to see that they are stained with a guilt that is not unlike that which they condemn in their enemies. Niebuhr has often assumed this role himself.

But a Christian may also be called to become a compromising statesman. He may hold high office in the land or he may be a private in the army. But wherever he is he knows that the perfect life is not a possibility for him. He knows that if he does not compromise and work for the lesser evil, a worse evil will triumph. He does not like the compromise; he constantly seeks the forgiveness of God for it; but he also feels that it is his duty to God to stand where he is and do the best that can be done in a complex situation. The majority of Christians will always be here. But despite the compromise, there is a world of difference between the Christian who accepts the compromise with sorrow and repentance and the man who compromises by accepting the evil as his good. The Christian will ever be alert to find some way to ameliorate the evil that he must do, while the other man will not even be conscious that he is involved in evil.

We might illustrate this difference by pointing with Niebuhr to Lincoln. Lincoln accepted the Civil War as a tragic necessity, the lesser of the two evils from which he had to choose. But because he knew that it was an evil, Lincoln had his heart open to forgive and to rehabilitate at the first opportunity. Over against Lincoln were those who fought what they considered was a righteous crusade and who had no idea that they were compromising. Their hearts were filled with a vindictive desire for vengeance. The difference in attitude made a world of difference for future history.

Niebuhr, more than any other, raised America above the impasse of the fundamentalist-modernist controversy by daring to see values and errors on both sides. If Americans and Europeans are able to converse with each other in the ecumenical movement, it is partly because Niebuhr has been a mediator between them. Today one does not often find references to Niebuhr in theology and many of the younger theologians like to think that they have moved beyond him. It may become apparent in the future, however, that they have not gone beyond Niebuhr, they have gone around him and are busy falling into the same pitfalls of optimism and irrelevance that Niebuhr criticized so cogently in the thirties and forties.

8

The Boundary Between Liberalism and Neo-Orthodoxy: Paul Tillich

Born in 1886, Tillich was the son of a Prussian pastor. He was educated under the influence of nineteenth century liberalism to which he brought a mystical appreciation of nature. During the First World War he was a chaplain in the German army where he came fact to face with deep social problems. After the war he became a professor of theology and began to work with the Religious Socialist movement, an activity that made life under Hitler impossible. In 1933, with the aid of Reinhold Niebuhr, he fled from Germany to become a professor at Union Theological Seminary, New York. At the age of forty-seven he began a new career in a new country with a new language. After a few years he became known as one of America's greatest theologians. In 1955 he retired from Union and became University Professor of theology at Harvard. After a lifetime as a seminary professor he met the challenge of speaking to undergraduates so well that his classes were always packed. To the end he kept on working and, when he died in 1965, he was still teaching at the University of Chicago.

Tillich has been called, with good reason, the "theologian's theologian." His writings are never easy reading. He brought to his work an amazing scholarship. He was completely at home in several fields of thought, including history, philosophy, psychology, and art, in addition to theology. He was typical of German scholarship at its best. He recalled without effort the essence of the though of the most obscure thinker of the past. But, also typical of the scholar, he could not, without the aid of his assistant, recall where he had left his lecture notes.

For several years Tillich occupied a strange position in theology. In Europe he was widely looked upon as a liberal theologian in active opposition to Barth and Brunner. He sometimes referred humorously to himself as the "last liberal." But when he came to America he was considered a spokesman of neo-orthodoxy. He frequently claimed that he stood on the boundary between liberalism and neo-orthodoxy. He joined the liberals in their insistence that religion must be subjected to the scrutiny of reason. He accepted wholeheartedly the higher criticism of the Bible and was deeply concerned to relate religion and culture. On the other hand, he aligned himself with neo-orthodoxy in his insistence that the final criterion of all revelation is the picture of "Jesus as the Christ" which we find in the Bible. As the years passed it became evident that Tillich had developed a theological system that defied attempts to put it into any category. In an eclectic spirit he drew on several secular philosophies and a great variety of theologies but as the material went through his hands it appeared in a fresh light.

Central to Tillich's system is the "principle of correlation." Tillich argues that it is the unavoidable duty of every theologian to relate the bibilical message to his contemporary situation. He insists that man cannot receive answers to questions that he has not even asked. Therefore, if man is to understand the revelation of Christ, there must be a preparation which enables him to comprehend revelation, that is, there must be a correlation between the thought and problems of man and the answers given by religious faith. It is the task of the theologian to demonstrate this correlation. In other words, Christian theology must learn to speak the language of the culture in which it finds itself.

Each section of Tillich's *Systematic Theology* begins with an analysis of a particular problem in terms of philosophy. When the problem has been probed to its final depth and its relation to man's existence and being becomes clear, Tillich shows how the Christian revelation gives an answer to the problem. The answer is always symbolic and even paradoxical, but it is ultimately more satisfying than any alternative.

Tillich does not imply by his method of correlation that the answers to the problems of life can be deduced from the philosophical analysis of them. The answers are supplied "from beyond." Tillich tries to stand between what he considers to be two false methods. On the one hand, naturalistic philosophy tries to answer questions from the analysis of man's natural existence. This method fails to see that it is man's existence itself which is the question. Liberal theology often makes the error of explaining Christianity as a system developed by man's natural religious tendencies. Christianity thus becomes something that is said by man, not something said to man. On the other hand, Tillich repudiates what he calls the supernaturalistic fallacy which sees the Christian message as a set of sacred truths that "have fallen into the human situation like strange bodies from a strange world."

The method of correlation becomes more clear when we understand three terms that Tillich uses continually: theonomy, heteronomy, and autonomy. All thinking, believes Tillich, is an expression of one or more of these.

Heteronomy is the imposition of a law upon man from outside himself. Heteronomy may appear in religious or secular forms. When a religion sets itself up to dictate belief and action, it is heteronomous. It ignores and destroys all creativity within man; it stifles the expression of man's reason. Heteronomy usually justifies itself by claiming to speak for God. In heteronomy God is pictured as the supreme lawgiver who must be obeyed simply because he demands. Why should we obey such a God? Only, it would seem, says Tillich, because he is more powerful than we. But this is a poor reason, for we destroy ourselves in submitting to such a strange and alien power.

When men have been subjected to a heteronomy, sooner or later they rebel, and usually they rebel in the name of autonomy, the rule of the self by the self. In autonomy one lives by the rational structure of his own mind, making his own laws. The autonomous man is one who refuses to bow before anything outside himself, and who sets out to be the captain of his fate and the master of his soul.

Theonomy repudiates both heteronomy and autonomy. It asserts that the superior law, rooted in God, is at the same time the innermost law of man himself. One does not receive this law from external agencies but finds it within his own heart. The law given by God is thus in harmony with man's own essential nature. It calls man to be what he was meant to be. In obeying the law of God theonomously, one does not destroy himself as when he obeys a heteronomous law; rather he fulfills himself. He finds what he truly is. The commands of God are to be fulfilled, then, not because God has more power than we but because they are the expression of man's essential relation to himself, to others, and to the universe.

As Tillich looks back over history he finds that different historical periods have been characterized by one or the other of these forms. The early Middle Ages and the early Reformation were periods of theonomy when the ultimate depth of life, God, shone through everything. Religion is a natural expression of life in the theonomous period. There is no division of life into sacred and secular, for all life is seen in its relation to the divine. In such a society religion does not stand over man giving him orders; rather it is the lifeblood of one's existence, the presupposition of all thought. Men are not even consciously religious. In theonomous periods men do not feel split; instead they feel whole, centered, and at home in the universe.

When a theonomous period loses its power, it normally sinks into heteronomy. When the religious life is no longer that which comes naturally, the religious authorities try to force men to be religious. Thought must be censored, misdeeds punished, and the law of God enforced by the proper authorities. Thus the late Middle Ages and the later period of the Reformation both developed heteronomies. Orthodoxy became a strict rule to be enforced; religious persecution became common.

The reaction to a heteronomous period is often a period of autonomy. The Renaissance reacted autonomously to the late Middle Ages, and Rationalism, in the eighteenth century, reacted to the heteronomous othodoxy of later Protestantism. There is no doubt that Tillich welcomes the autonomous revolt; it is perfectly proper against the demands of heteronomy. Autonomy fights heteronomy for the freedom and dignity of the individual. The autonomous period throws aside all external rule. It sets up principles such as "Art for art's sake," "Business is business," and "One man's religion is as good as another's."

Although Tillich applauds the reassertion of autonomy against heteronomy, he finds that the autonomous period cannot satisfy the deeper needs of man. It leaves him without any depth or cohesion in life. We stand today in the midst of a disintegrating autonomous order. An autonomous age loses both its view of the world as a whole and a center to life. Life is split into a series of unrelated activities with no depth or meaning. The autonomous man becomes bewildered, with no direction to life. He is no longer self-assured and creative, but disturbed, frustrated, and often in despair. In short, autonomy gives man no certainty, no security, and no foundation for life.

When an autonomous period breaks down, as it is doing today, it may go in one of two directions. The lure of heteronomy is strong at such a time. Religions of authoritarianism offer man a sense of security and strength if he will give up his autonomous freedom. On the other hand, secular heteronomies arise in the form of totalitarian states, whether Nazi or Communist, offering men the sense of a unified life, a meaningful goal for the future, and above all security. We live in an age that leads many to "escape from freedom." The other alternative is that a new theonomy may arise. Men on the borderline of despair may, instead of abandoning their freedom, find the wholeness, meaning, and depth of life in God. God in such theonomy is not an outside force or power that comes in to rescue man; God is the depth and foundation behind those aspects of truth and goodness which autonomy has already found.

Theonomy is expressed for Tillich in the essential principle of Protestantism. His understanding of Protestantism begins with an analysis of man. Man finds himself faced with a "boundary situation" which arises at the point where everything that makes life meaningful is threatened. It is encountered whenever all human possibility reaches its limit or boundary. At this point existence itself is threatened. This is not to be confused with death, although death may point to man's boundary situation.

The boundary situation is a threat to man because

of his freedom. Man does not grow, as does a flower, into his natural form; he has freedom to decide for or against it. He is haunted with the demand to fulfill the good and the true. If this demand is not fulfilled, and it never is, then life is driven into discord, guilt, and ultimately to anxiety. Man tries in various ways to escape this anxiety. He leans upon past success in finding truth or in achieving goodness. He runs to the arms of a heteronomous religion which promises him security. He may throw himself into restless activity or sink in the delights of the flesh. He may try to find his security in totalitarian political movements. At the end of an autonomous era like ours, man is threshing about looking in all directions for salvation from the threat to the meaning and value of his existence.

The anxiety faced at the boundary is not to be identified with fear. Fear is always directed at a specific danger and may be overcome by courage. But anxiety is the underlying and deeper sense of insecurity that comes from realizing that the whole end and meaning of our existence are threatened. So it is that man finds a sense of relief when, for brief periods, he can lose his anxiety in fear of some specific threat to himself. Then he can muster up his courage and face the threat; but this is always a temporary expedient and, sooner or later, he must again find himelf on the boundary. Likewise, this anxiety is not to be confused with neurotic fear and anxiety that can be cured by psychotherapy. This anxiety is the mark of human nature as such.

The Protestant principle is the answer of Christianity, says Tillich, to the boundary situation of life.

Protestantism grew out of Luther's rediscovery of the biblical message of justification by faith. This is the paradox that man, the unrighteous, is accepted by God as if he were righteous; man, the unholy, is accepted as if he were holy. Man's anxiety and feeling of guilt are overcome when he accepts the fact that God has accepted him as he is. No longer does he need to pretend that he is more than he is; he can face all of the ambiguity of the boundary situation without rationalizing it away. Man's need to deceive himself is removed. Man's whole life is transformed by the acceptance of God.

The faith by which one receives the forgiving grace of God is not less certain knowledge. Faith means being grasped by the sense of the unconditional which is beyond man. In faith one is lifted out of himself; he is gripped by a power not his own. The saint is not a saint because he is good; he is a saint because he has become transparent for that which is more than himself.

Because of its understanding of grace, Protestantism represents the eternally necessary protest against everything that is set up to take the place of God. To Protestantism only God is holy, and no Church, no doctrine, no saint, no institution, no rite, is holy in itself. Each of these is holy only insofar as it may become a symbol that points beyond itself to the divine holiness. Protestantism revolted from the Roman Catholic Church because the latter claimed that it, as an institution, had the power of dispensing God's grace. The Protestant principle must likewise protest against even a Protestant Church or creed when it claims to speak absolutely for God. Protestantism is in unqualified opposition to all heteronomy. Wherever heteronomy arises in Protestant garb, it is a perversion of Protestantism. The Protestant is thus led to insist on the priesthood of all believers; that is, the grace of God is not channeled through any particular group of ordained men but is open to all. In any given period the Churches may be so closed to God that he has to work through a purely secular movement. Therefore the duty of Protestantism is not to condemn secularism in unqualified terms; rather it is to stimulate the secularists to look more deeply into their thought and to find its ground and depth, to lead them to the awareness of the theonomous nature of their thought and life.

Tillich feels certain that we are living at the end of an era. The social forces and thought forms that have governed life for the past few centuries are in disintegration. The problem of the Protestant Church is that it is so closely identified with the decaying society that it faces the real possibility of dying with the old order. The Protestant principle may have to express itself elsewhere and in opposition to the official Protestant Churches.

For Tillich religion is not a matter of certain beliefs or practices; it cannot be identified with the traditional religions. A man is religious at the point where he is ultimately concerned, and he is ultimately concerned when he experiences the unconditional. The experience of the unconditional is the experience of that which has absolute authority for one, of that before which he bows in humility and awe. Ethical obligation, the striving for truth, and beauty, all have elements of the unconditional in them. An ultimate concern is one that takes precedence over all of the other concerns of life. The ultimate concern grasps a man and lifts him out of himself. To it he says, "Not my will but thy will be done." He gives himself to it with all of his heart and mind and soul and strength. An ultimate concern is total; there is no part of oneself or of one's world that is excluded from it.

When one understands religion in these terms, it is evident that religion is often found among the so-called "irreligious." The atheist usually has an ultimate concern for truth or for some other reality. In fact, says Tillich, we must realize that the atheist may be saved by faith. His atheism may arise from a commitment to, and ultimate concern with, truth. Loyalty to truth will not allow him to believe in the God pictured by a religion. But his loyalty to truth is itself a relationship to God, although the atheist does not recognize it as such.

This definition of religion makes it clear that our problem is not irreligion but false religion. Idolatry, the giving of one's ultimate concern to that which is neither ultimate nor unconditional, is the source of the world's ills. When men give their ultimate concern to their state, their Church, their political party, or any other preliminary concern, the results are destructive and chaotic.

The object of theology is that, and only that, which concerns us ultimately. The conflict of science and theology has occurred either when the theologians tried to pontificate on matters of preliminary concern or when the scientist tried to dictate about ultimate concern. Theology has nothing to say about questions of science, art, history, and so on. The preliminary concerns come into theological consideration only when they become symbols pointing toward the ultimate concern.

Because of the nature of religion, theology can never be simply and purely objective. There are, Tillich insists, areas where the detached and objective approach is most satisfactory. But to apply this method, so satisfactory in the physical sciences, to all fields of knowledge is to be less than truly objective. Unconcerned detachment in matters of religion implies an a priori rejection of the religious demand to be ultimately concerned. Hence it denies the God whom it claims to be approaching objectively.

But, we may ask, what ought to concern us ultimately? Tillich replies, "Our ultimate concern is that which determines our being or non-being." We become ultimately concerned with that which we believe to have the power of destroying or saving our very being. Tillich hastens to point out that he does not have in mind our physical being. Many things threaten or save our physical life without concerning us ultimately. He uses the term "being" to refer to the whole of human reality, the structure, the meaning, and the aim of existence. "To be or not to be" in this sense is a matter of ultimate concern. It penetrates to the very depth of the meaning of life, why we live and for what we live.

In view of the nature of the ultimate concern, Tillich finds that the popular idea of God is not worthy of ultimate concern. This God is but an idol. So Tillich startled his hearers by telling them that he did not believe that God exists. He repudiated the "so-called proofs" for the "so-called existence" of God. This strategy was partly intended to shock his listeners into attention, and it was partly for the sake of more precise terminology.

For Tillich, God does not exist because existence is a category of dependence. A god who exists is simply another being, and even if we call him the supreme being he is still on the same level with ourselves. Superlatives become diminutives when applied to God because they compare God to other beings. This pulls God down to our level even while ostensibly trying to raise him up. Such a god is not worthy of our ultimate concern; he may be more powerful than we, he may be able to blot out our physical existence, but he cannot concern our true existence, the meaning, purpose, and goal of our life. Instead of looking outside nature for a supernatural being called God, Tillich looks through nature to the transcendent depth and ground of nature. God, says Tillich, is not a being, he is Being itself, the power of being which enables all things that are to be.

The history of religion is full of gods. Gods, says Tillich, are beings of superhuman powers. Though they are greater than men, they are images of human nature raised to a superhuman realm. This causes certain skeptics to charge that the gods are only projections of human nature. That is true, says Tillich, but the skeptic forgets that something projected must be projected onto something, a screen. In this case the screen is the experience of a realm that is of ultimate concern.

The sphere of the gods is the sphere of the holy. Holiness is an experienced phenomenon. The holy is the quality of that which concerns man ultimately, and only that which is holy can give one ultimate concern. The experience of holiness is normally evoked by some object, and the peril of religion is that the object, which is the occasion of the experience, is taken to be holy itself. Thus arise idolatries in which the objects of religion are considered divine and holy in themselves.

The various attempts to prove the existence of God are perverse, believes Tillich, for they deny God in the very attempt to prove him. Every argument for the existence of God uses God as a missing link to explain the world as we know it. But to call this missing link God is the worst form of atheism. The arguments for the existence of God are not arguments nor are they proofs of God's existence. They are valid only as an analysis of man's situation. Man asks the question about God because he is already aware of God. This awareness is not the result of the argument; it is the presupposition with which it begins. All of the arguments point to the presence of something unconditional within the self and the world. Without this the question would not be asked.

Man faces this unconditional element in the sense of truth. Even the skeptic who says there is no truth has expressed his faith in truth—the truth of his statement that there is no truth. The demand of truth presents itself as unconditional. Man cannot be satisfied with less. Similarly, the sense of ought, the demand to be good, is an unconditional demand. A man may or may not do the good, but he cannot escape the fact that it lays its claims upon him and challenges him.

When we speak of God we must speak, says Tillich, in symbolic terms. The only nonsymbolic statement we can make about God is that he is Being itself. He is not a being but he is that power of being which is within every being enabling it to exist and without which it would cease to exist. Everything else we can say about God is symbolic. For example, we must speak of God as personal, for man cannot be ultimately concerned with anything less than personal. But such a statement is symbolic, for personality implies limitation. It is none the less a fitting symbol, for God is the power of being that underlies all personality and makes it what it is. Similarly, we speak of God causing certain things, but this too is symbolic. God is the basis upon which causality rests, without which there would be neither cause nor effect. But the ground of causation cannot properly be called a cause, not even a First Cause. The world is not something apart from God; it is the medium of his continuing activity.

Faith in God is the answer to the search for a courage that is able to overcome the anxiety that arises from man's boundary situation that we examined earlier. Ordinary courage may overcome the specific threats, but a deeper courage is necessary to overcome the anxiety that arises from the finite nature of life itself. This deeper or ultimate courage is based upon participation in the ultimate power of being. The finitude and the anxiety do not disappear, but the power to live with them is found.

Throughout this discussion of Tillich's view of God, it is evident that Tillich depends upon a deep sense of mysticism. God is experienced as the unconditioned within life. Nature is not simply many objects outside oneself; it is a transparent window through which one can see the reality of God. God is experienced as the sustainer of nature and of oneself—the power from which one draws ultimate courage and a transformation of life. God can never be, therefore, an object beside other objects; he is the depth of reality from which all objects draw their reality.

Tillich combines faith in the finality of revelation in Christ with a sympathetic appreciation of revelation in other religions. The Christian faith that Christ reveals the truth includes the claim that wherever truth appears it is in harmony with Christ. The message of Christ would not have been understood if there had not been a preparation for it. It would have fallen as a strange and meaningless phenomenon in a world that had no prior revelation. The religions of man, including the Christian religion, are the preparations enabling man to comprehend the "New Being" that comes in Christ.

Jesus as the Christ was a "New Being" in the sense that he portrayed completely what God meant man to be. Man, as he exists in this world, is not man as God created him to be. This is the meaning of the fall for Tillich; there is a split between the essence of man, what God intended him to be, and what man is ex-

istentially (that is, is in reality). In Jesus we find man
in complete unity with God, meeting the vicissitudes
and temptations of human life but overcoming them
with the grace of God. Jesus is not the Christ because
of his own power or goodness but because God was
present in him. As such the Christian claims that
Christ is the final revelation. This does not mean that
revelation ceased in the year 33, but it does mean that
all revelations are to be tested and weighed by the
revelation that comes through Christ.

This claim to finality is justified by Tillich because
in Jesus we find a revelation with the power to negate
itself without losing itself. Every revelation from the
infinite God must come through some medium, but
this means that the medium blurs the revelation or in
many cases takes the place of the revelation. It is the
wonder of Jesus that he gave up all claims for himself;
he surrendered everything that was Jesus in him to
that which was Christ. That is, Jesus made no personal demands or claims; he pointed continually to
God, who worked in and through him. Because Jesus
surrendered himself so completely, he became transparent to the mystery that he revealed. Jesus' temptations were the temptations to claim ultimacy for his
own finite nature. Jesus steadfastly resisted all temptations to use his union with God for his own advantage.

For Tillich this makes a "Jesus-centered" religion
idolatrous. He believes that liberal theology often fell
into this error. It is not Jesus the man whom we worship, but the mystery of God that shines through him.
Christians do not set up Jesus as a heteronomous au-

thority who demands obedience. Rather in Jesus as the Christ we find the answer to the questions asked in all of men's religions about the relation of man to the ultimate and to his fellow men. In Christ we find not a new law but the true nature of man.

Christianity has no superiority over other religions as a religion. Its people are no more righteous than those of other faiths. But that to which Christianity witnesses, the picture of the Christ, is final.

The revelation of Christ emphasizes love as the law of life. Love in the Christian sense is a power rather than an emotion—the power that reunites that which has been separated. Love combines the sense of an absolute ought with the relativity necessary for particular situations. In every situation in which another person is involved, we ought to treat him with love. But how love will act in any particular situation will depend upon the individual needs of the persons involved. Love is not a heteronomous law; it expresses itself in terms of individual needs.

Tillich notes that whereas a few years ago the dominant problem was the control of nature, today it is the problem of history. Much of his work has been in this field. He finds that though men have freedom in historical situations, there is also a power of destiny that limits the possibilities in any given period. History is going someplace; it has an end and is not a meaningless repetition of events. Within history there is the continual struggle between the forces of good and evil, a struggle that divides both the individual and society. The meaning of history is found in the revelation of Christ.

Tillich has used a term, *kairos,* to describe the opportunities of history. This is a Greek word used by Paul with regard to Christ and is translated "in the fullness of time." Tillich finds here the concept that the time was ready or prepared for the invasion of history by God through Christ. It was the one unique moment when the revelation was possible. Sooner or later would not have been adequate. As there was the one great *kairos* when Christ came, there are, believes Tillich, smaller *kairoi* throughout history when the time is ripe for particular achievements. The hour of destiny strikes for some new social creation.

The concept of *kairos* enables Tillich to stand between two extremes. On the one hand, he repudiates the pessimist who sees no hope for the future history of man or who believes that no progress is possible. On the other hand, he rejects any form of utopianism which would claim to have built or to be able to build a perfect earthly society. Tillich believes that in the *kairos* a particular gain may be made, a battle with evil won, but that the victory will not be an absolute one over all evils.

It is Tillich's belief that we stand today in a *kairos.* With an era decaying around us, we have an opportunity to build a new theonomous period. In the light of this we can understand his concept of religious socialism. He finds that socialism is acutely aware that we stand in a *kairos* period, that an old age is dying, and that a new one is waiting to be born. Religious socialism is not a political movement; it is an attempt to understand socialism under the light of theonomy. It is as critical of socialism as it is of capitalism. It is not sympathetic either to Marxism or to Communism.

Socialism, says Tillich, sees clearly and rightly the evils of capitalism, the injustices, unemployment, and mechanization of the worker. But socialism fails to go deeply enough in its criticism. Like the capitalists socialists hope to change society simply by changing techniques and strategy. Like capitalism, socialism tends to make the highest possible increase in economic welfare into its all-determining goal. In this way socialism becomes but the other side of the coin of capitalism, the competitor of capitalism, but not its true alternative.

Tillich's religious socialism tried to understand the divine ground of the social and economic situation. On the other hand, it realized, as much orthodox Christianity did not, that the social conditions of an era can be a real hindrance to the spiritual welfare of man. It also recognized that, to an alarming extent, Protestantism had become the religious aspect of capitalism. The proletariat were estranged from the Protestant Church. Religious socialism set itself the task of winning the proletariat by accepting all that was just and true in the socialist philosophy and pointing to the deeper truths missed by secular socialism. On the other hand, it criticized the utopianism that was evident in socialism. For the religious socialist the *kairos* of socialism has come, but socialism is not and could not be the Kingdom of God or the perfect and final social order. The failure of Marxian Communism to understand this is in large part responsible for its falling into a new and demonic form of heteronomy.

Tillich was a deep and complex thinker. He can no more be summarized in one chapter such as this than can an encyclopedia. It can only be hoped that we have pointed to something of the uniqueness, breadth, and depth of his thought. In recent years Tillich's thought has been subjected to considerable study by both Protestant and Roman Catholic theologians. There is not, however, a school of thought which could be called Tillichian. To many of the younger theologians his thought is too metaphysical for an age that thinks of itself as post-metaphysical. It is too soon to prophecy whether Tillich has made an enduring theological contribution or whether he simply explored and marked on the map a theological dead end. Without doubt the future of Tillichian thought will depend upon whether or not metaphysical systems again come into fashion.

9

Rudolf Bultmann:
Radical Conservative

For the past decade or so the most influential theologian in Europe and, to a lesser degree, in America, has been Rudolf Bultmann. Born in 1884, Bultmann first became known as a New Testament scholar who was influenced by Barth's theology. Most of his career was spent in teaching at Marburg. He was a member of the Confessing Church under the Nazis but, unlike Tillich and Barth, he was able to remain in his teaching position. This was no doubt because, as he says, he never participated in political affairs. During the Second World War Bultmann published a forty-page essay entitled "New Testament and Mythology," which catapulted him into the center of theological controversy and introduced into theology the term "demythologization." Although Bultmann retired from his professorship in 1951, his years of greatest influence have come during his retirement because of the debate his essay stimulated. We can understand Bultmann best, however, if we do not begin with his concept of demythologization. A great deal of misunderstanding has arisen from the failure to interpret Bultmann's controversial essay in light of his total thought.

Bultmann has remained rooted in the insights of early neo-orthodoxy. There is, he affirms, a qualitative difference between God and the world. No philosophical analysis of the world can produce any knowledge of God. God is known only in his revelation of himself but even there he is hidden so that no rational or empirical study of the revealing events can find revelation. Revelation is seen only with the eyes of faith. Bultmann applies the concept of justification through faith alone to knowledge as well as to salvation. If no work can earn our salvation, neither can any intellectual work prove that we are dealing with God. God is not an object for human thought, we cannot speak objectively about God and thus Bultmann repudiates Tillich's identification of God with Being Itself.

Because God cannot be an object for man to study, we cannot speak of God unless, says Bultmann, we speak also about ourselves. To know God is to be changed and thus to speak of God is to speak of what God has done for me. At first sight it may seem that theology does say certain things about God apart from God's relationship to man. For example, we say that God created the universe. But, says Bultmann, the doctrine of creation is not a cosmological theory about the origin of the universe. If I confess that I believe in God as Creator I am expressing a sense of my finiteness and my faith that the origin of myself and my world lies outside of myself and my world. Creation is not a description of a past event but a recognition that my present life is "uncanny," that is, it is filled with a sense of awe and dread. It affirms that I am more than just another thing in the world of things; I am not just the product of a causal series, but rather I am a free agent who is called to make decisions. Finally it is my confession that my whole life is limited both in time and in power and that I am ultimately responsible for who I am.

Bultmann's theology is closely related to his historical scholarship. He was one of the New Testament scholars who led in the development of what is known as "form criticism." The form critic attempts to go behind written documents to the time when the tradition was handed down by word of mouth. Form criticism believes that there are laws governing the development of oral traditions. To aid memory, stories are put into certain patterns. If the reader examines the Gospels he will find that stories of miracles or controversies usually have similar forms. Because oral traditions tend to develop in certain ways over a period of time, the form critic hopes to separate earlier from later traditions and to identify points that have been added to a story as it was retold.

A basic step for the form critic is to analyze the community which preserved, told, and finally wrote the stories as we have them. What was the life situation and problems that led the early Church to tell a story in the form in which we now have it? At first sight it seems that form criticism has abandoned all hope of discovering anything about Jesus for it is only able to learn about the Church which told stories about Jesus. And Bultmann does insist that we cannot discover the historical Jesus. A study of the Gospels shows that their writers had no interest in history as

we think of it. They were not scholars bent on preserving the past; they were preaching to the world
about the Lord and Savior in whom man may find
new life. Bultmann, however, does not feel that this
should cause us to despair of learning anything about
Jesus. For one thing, form criticism shows that some
of the Gospel records are authentic history, particularly those that relate the teaching of Jesus. Furthermore, the Church came into being only because of
Jesus and thus his spirit breathes through it. In the
Gospels we do not get a video-tape of the life of Jesus,
but we do see vividly how he affected those who knew,
loved, and followed him.

To some theologians it seems that form criticism's
doubts about the historical validity of the Gospels
would destroy the Christian faith. Is not Christianity
based upon what God did in history? Thus many attack form criticism by pointing out that its methods
are imprecise and that form critics seldom agree with
each other. But for Bultmann this kind of objection
misses the whole point. To Bultmann, the concern to
verify the historicity of the Gospel accounts of Jesus'
life is another form of trying to save oneself by works.
It may seem that if we historically verify the events
related in the Gospels, we will somehow have proven
Christianity to be true. But, argues Bultmann, nothing that could be proved historically could prove that
Jesus was the risen Son of God who is preached by the
Church. Most of those who saw Jesus during his life
did not believe in him so why should historical proof
today make him any more believable than he was in
his lifetime?

Bultmann says that we need to reexamine the whole question of history and its relationship to Christian faith. We tend too easily to see history under the same kind of "subject-object" cleavage with which we approach things in the world. That is, the scientist, for example, takes a purely subject-object approach to a chemical that he is studying; he looks at it from outside and analyzes it objectively. But we cannot do this with history because the historian is a part of history. True history is never simply an account which states objectively that certain events happened. True history seeks always to find the meaning of events. It is a fact that on November 22, 1963, President Kennedy was shot in Dallas. But the flow of books about that incident proves that the bare fact is not enough. Men long to see its meaning in terms of the persons involved, their motives and emotional reactions. Thus Bultmann affirms that true history requires that the historian enter into dialogue with the history that he studies; it must come alive again for him.

Christian faith is not concerned with Jesus as a past event in history. As such, Jesus is just another martyred hero. Christian faith is interested only in the risen Christ who brings new life to man as he is met today in the words of preaching and in the sacraments of the Church. The important thing about the Gospels is not that they tell us about Jesus "as he really was," whatever that might mean, but that they show us what Jesus meant to the first Christians and thus what he can mean to us.

Bultmann is concerned with how men today can understand the Bible as a Word addressed to *them*. If we are to understand any writing, he says, we must have a "pre-understanding." Thus, if a book makes reference to musical terminology, it will be meaningless to us unless we already know something about music. But how can we have a pre-understanding of the Bible when it speaks of God and Bultmann argues that, apart from revelation, we cannot know God? Bultmann replies that we do know, as human beings, the questions to which God is the answer. Frequently Bultmann refers to Augustine's statement that our hearts are restless until they find rest in God. Man may not use the term God but he is aware that he is not what he ought to be; he is aware that he lacks fulfillment; he knows that he is moving toward death. To man, with this self-awareness, the Word of God comes as the answer to his implicit questions. In revelation we find that God is both our limit and the one who frees us from limitations.

Since to understand the New Testament we need a pre-understanding of what it means to be a human being, theology must draw upon a philosophical analysis of what it means to be man. Here Bultmann turns to the philosophy of Martin Heidegger. Heidegger attempted, in his book *Being and Time,* to analyze what it means to be a man. Heidegger's philosophy is complicated and many philosophers have found it beyond comprehension. We shall not attempt here to summarize Heidegger; we shall limit ourselves to the points that Bultmann draws from him.

In Heidegger, Bultmann finds a philosophy that gives him the tools for understanding human nature. Heidegger does not provide Bultmann with any knowledge of God or of revelation, but he does provide that pre-understanding which man needs if he is to understand the New Testament. Although Heidegger is not a Christian, Bultmann believes that Heidegger could not write as he does if there had never been the Christian faith. Heidegger owes much to Kierkegaard and thus to Luther and the New Testament. But what Heidegger says about man can be understood quite apart from Christian faith.

On the basis of Heidegger, Bultmann finds that to be human is to stand out from the rest of the world. Man is the being who, to exist, must have some understanding that he exists. The categories that we use to describe and to know things cannot be applied to man because man is not a thing with fixed characteristics. In a basic sense the self of man transcends the material world in which he finds himself and transcends even his own given nature of reason, emotions, etc. Herein lies man's freedom, his power to choose what he will be.

Man thus finds that he faces life with what Heidegger calls "care." This arises from man's recognition that he is free to choose what he will be. Man does not come with a predetermined set of properties like an acid or even an animal that is ruled by its instincts. On the other hand, man is forced to realize that he is surrounded by a situation that is not of his own choosing. He is "thrown" into existence without having a choice; he has a particular social and historical heritage, a particular set of abilities, etc. Man "falls" by losing himself in the world of things about him. He tries to deny his freedom and to become simply what his environment would make him. But even in his fallen state man cannot escape responsibility for himself.

Man is thus aware that he is faced with a twofold possibility—he can live authentically or inauthentically. Inauthentic living means that one allows himself to be determined by the world of things. Instead of deciding for himself he lets the crowd decide for him. But even as he lives inauthentically man cannot escape a sense that he is not fully at home in the world. He tries to find his security in things but there is no final security there. Because he knows that he did not bring himself into existence, he knows that he cannot choose when he shall pass out of existence. It will not do to say that death is natural and all men must die, for that will be of no comfort when I recognize that it is not *man* who is going to die, *I* am going to die. But, as I must die my death, so I must live my life. I must accept responsibility for it.

Authentic life occurs where man takes responsibility for himself. He is liberated from his past and open for his future. He is truly free. No longer is man under the tyranny of things; no longer is he guided by what the crowd expects of him. He dares to be himself. So long as man lives inauthentically he cannot be truly related to his fellowmen. On the one hand, as he seeks security through things, he finds that he is in competition with his neighbors for things. And insofar as he is a slave to the crowd's expectations, he must see others as a limitation upon his freedom. But when he lives authentically man is no longer so interested in things that he must compete with his neighbor. He accepts the limitations of being thrown into a particular situation and thus is free to love his neighbors instead of resenting the pressure they put upon him.

Bultmann finds that this philosophical analysis of what it means to be human is in harmony with the New Testament. When Paul describes man as a slave to the world, is this not the inauthentic life that is pictured by Heidegger? Is not Heidegger's concept of the fall like the biblical understanding of man's fall with Adam? Does this mean that Christianity is simply a form of existentialist philosophy or is existentialism a secularized Christianity? No, says Bultmann, philosophy can describe human existence and its possibilities but philosophy has no power to enable a man to *live* the authentic life. The philosopher thinks that man's conscience has the power to move him to authentic life. But this is to fail to take seriously the sin involved in man's fallen state. As the Bible emphasizes, we cannot save ourselves by our works. When man tries to reform himself he puts himself more firmly at the center of his world and into competition with his fellowmen. Man may see that authentic life is a life of love toward his neighbor but he cannot make himself love. He can only love as a response to a love that he receives.

The message of the Bible is that what man could not do for himself, God has done for him. In Christ God expresses his love to man and, when man accepts this love, he is freed to love others. When man hears that his sin is forgiven he is freed from his sinful past and made free for the future. When man recognizes that his existence is a gift from God, he is able to give it back to God. When he sees the world of things as God's creation, he is freed to use it without becoming dependent upon it. The Christian is not an ascetic who turns from the world of things. To do so would be inauthentic, for the man who must renounce the things of the world still gives them too much importance. The Christian way is expressed in I Corinthians 7:29–31. The key to the passage is that Christians are to have the things of the world "as though they had them not." That is, one uses them without being idolatrously bound up in them. Because one has been freed from anxiety he does not need such things to give him security.

There is another way in which Bultmann distinguishes Christian faith from a philosophical analysis. He uses the analogy of a man who longs to have a friend but does not have one. This man can know what a friend is and he can talk intelligently about friendship. Then the day comes when he makes a true friend. What does he know that he did not know before? He knows nothing more in terms of theoretical knowledge; he will still use the same words to describe friendship. And yet he is a different person because of his friendship. He lives his life in a new dimension, he sees himself and his friend in a way that he could not have seen before. He knows nothing more *about* friendship but he knows now what it is to be a friend. One thing that all of the psychology of friendship could never have told him is what his friend would *be* to him.

Whenever Bultmann speaks about God he soon begins to use analogies drawn from personal relationships because he believes that man's relationship to God is analogous to a man's relationship to other persons. Thus philosophy leaves us in the position of a man who knows all about friendship but who has no friend. Philosophy can speak about authentic life, it can see the promised land from afar, but it cannot know what it is to *be* authentic. This is known only when God's Word comes to us as a personal address. When God speaks and we respond with faith we do not learn some new theory about the world; we become new men, we pass from death to life. We do not simply hear that our sins have been forgiven—that would be a cold theory. We are in fact freed from sin.

Now we can see why Bultmann argues that an historical knowledge of the man Jesus is irrelevant to Christian faith. Knowledge about Jesus would be like knowledge about friendship—a theory without power in our lives. The Jesus of history would be, at best, an example to follow but as such he would drive us further into despair, for who can be like Jesus by his own effort? The Christ who saves us is the risen Lord whom we meet in our lives. And where do we meet this risen Lord? He comes to us hidden in the words of preaching and in the sacraments.

Bultmann's critics fear that he has made Christianity purely subjective. How can we know that our faith is not wishful thinking? Bultmann's answer is that we cannot know if by "know" we have in mind the way we can know that hydrogen and oxygen unite to form water. If one tries to find such objective truth he is sinking back into inauthentic life, trying to find security in the world of things. Like friendship, faith is a risk. We cannot prove objectively that our friend loves us, perhaps he is using us, but this does not mean that we are unjustified in trusting him. What cannot be known by an objective analysis of the situation can be known by the man who is in the situation. Our justification for affirming faith in Christ is that we have become new men through faith in him. We cannot possess knowledge of God; we can only again and again encounter God in our lives as his Word comes to us anew, just as we know our friend's love in our continuing life with him. Once more we are reminded that we cannot speak of God without speaking of man who meets God.

With this background we can turn to Bultmann's concept of demythologization as it is found in his famous essay, "New Testament and Mythology." He begins by noting that the New Testament comes to us in a mythological framework that alienates modern man. It pictures the universe as three-storied, with heaven above the earth and hell below. From both heaven and hell there come spirits to control human life. The order of nature is frequently disrupted by supernatural intervention. The end of the world is expected in the near future when Christ will return on the clouds to judge men. Jesus is pictured as a pre-existent being who dies a sacrificial death to make atonement for man's sins. This mythical picture is impossible for modern man to accept because today men think in terms of a totally different world view and we cannot choose our world view at will. Bultmann believes that it is impossible for a man who uses the modern hospital to believe in the New Testament miracles.

Bultmann is often interpreted as being primarily concerned with making Christianity acceptable to modern man. This is unfortunate because both believers and unbelievers are suspicious of the man who waters Christianity down so that it will be more acceptable to the skeptical. Yet nothing could be further from Bultmann's intentions. He is convinced that the Christian faith contains a major scandal for all men. Its scandal is that it declares that man is a sinner who can only be saved through God's unique act in Christ. The problem, however, as Bultmann sees it is that modern man never has to face this true scandal of the faith. Instead he is scandalized by its mythological form and discards it as a fairy tale without coming to grips with what it says about his existence. And so Bultmann asks whether myth is an integral part of Christian faith and answers that it is not. It is simply the world view of the time and place in which Christianity arose. Christian faith itself demands to be freed from the mythical framework in which it began.

Bultmann says that the purpose of myth in the New Testament is not to present an objective picture of the world but to express man's understanding of himself. In myth man expresses his conviction that the origin and purpose of the world are to be found beyond the world. But myth uses imagery and terms taken from this world to express this conviction and this leads to contradiction. For example, myth tries to express the fact that God transcends the space-time world and so it speaks of God in spatial terms as "high and lifted up" but this draws God into our space-time system and makes him a being up in the sky. So, argues Bultmann, in the New Testament we find that the writers are beginning to overcome myth. John's Gospel drops the idea of Christ's second coming and pictures judgment coming upon the world with Jesus himself and eternal life as a reality into which man enters here and now.

Bultmann points out that in all ages theologians have wrestled with the problem of myth. Some, for example, have interpreted mythological passages as allegories of the inner life of the soul. Liberal theology attempted to get rid of mythology but its error was that, in doing so, it threw out the Gospel itself. Liberals lost the New Testament faith that in Christ God acted to save men. For them the New Testament was just another, perhaps the best, expression of universal truths of ethics and religion.

What then are we to do with New Testament myth? We must interpret it existentially, that is, we must try to see what was the understanding of their own existence that the New Testament writers were communicating through the myths. The term "demythologization" is not well chosen to describe Bultmann's purpose. The term leads us to expect Bultmann to get rid of myth whereas his concern is to interpret it in terms of man's existence. Thus he finds that the mythical language about Adam, "the flesh," and the demonic forces are ways of expressing man's experience of living inauthentically within the sphere of things. On the other hand, the New Testament references to the life of the spirit or being "in Christ" are descriptions of the authentic life.

Bultmann sees a unique problem in the life of Jesus because it is pictured in both mythical and historical terms. Jesus is pictured as a carpenter whose parents are known and yet he is a pre-existent being. He lived a human life and died a human death and yet we are told that he was born of a virgin. How do we reconcile such statements? In some cases, believes Bultmann, the problem is simple. The Virgin Birth stories are mythical attempts to express the meaning of Jesus for faith. They say that Christ comes to us as the action of God.

But what about the Cross and the Resurrection? The Cross is a fact of history but it is interpreted in a mythical way as the atoning sacrifice for the sins of the world. This cannot do justice to the Cross: at best it can tell us that all sins are forgiven. But the New Testament says much more than this. The Cross releases us not simply from punishment for sin; it releases us from the power of sin. Thus the Cross is not simply an event of past history; it is an ever-present event that comes to us in the sacraments. To receive the Cross today is to be crucified with Christ, to die to sin. Through the Cross we lose our natural dread of suffering; we are able to accept what comes to us in the world "as if we had it not." In the Cross judgment is passed on the world and that means that judgment is passed on me, and yet in this judgment I find deliverance. The Cross has created a new situation in history; it has opened new possibilities to man. When it is preached the Cross challenges men to accept the Cross for themselves and to be crucified with Christ.

The Cross, as we read about it in history, cannot bear this power to renew the lives of men. But when the Cross is preached it is never alone; it is linked to the resurrection of Jesus. But is not the Resurrection a mythical event pure and simple? Can we believe in the resuscitation of a corpse? Bultmann is concerned that we do not treat the Resurrection as a myth. Insofar as the New Testament does this, we must transcend the New Testament. We treat the Resurrection as a myth when we try to use it as a supernatural proof that Jesus was the Savior and that his death was a saving event for man. But this is doomed to fail because belief in the Resurrection is itself an article of faith and we cannot prove one article of faith by another. Furthermore, the attempt to use the Resurrection as a proof of Christ's divinity is again to fall into the inauthentic attitude which finds security in the objective world of things. The risen Christ comes to us in the words of preaching and calls us to faith. There is no way that history can prove the Resurrection. Just as I cannot prove to a skeptic that my friend loves me but can only know my friend's love in the relationship of love, so we cannot prove to the skeptic that Jesus rose from the dead. We can only meet the risen Christ in the preaching of the Church.

Consequently, for Bultmann the Resurrection means the rise of faith in the saving power of Christ's Cross. Christians participate in Christ's resurrection when they participate in his crucifixion. In this resurrection-life they enjoy a freedom, albeit a struggling and imperfect freedom, from sin. Without the knowledge of the saving power of the Cross, Jesus' death is simply the tragic death of another great man. But the saving power of the Cross means that Christ conquered death and has freed us from it. This power meets us in the words of preaching and thus Bultmann concludes that the faith of Easter is faith in the word of preaching.

Once more the voice of the critic is heard asking if we do not need some historical verification of all of this. How did faith in a resurrected Christ arise? What of the empty tomb? Bultmann replies that again we are seeking security in the objective world of things. All that historical research can prove for us is that the disciples came to believe in the Resurrection so that they went out to preach it. This will not persuade the skeptic. He can still try to explain it psychologically. But the man who would try to prove the Resurrection historically is missing the whole point. Easter faith means the same thing for us that it did for the first disciples—the self-manifestation of the risen Lord through whom the redemptive event of the Cross is made complete. There is an old Gospel hymn with the chorus,

> He lives, he lives,
> Salvation to impart.
> You ask me how I know he lives—
> He lives within my heart.

Strangely enough, Bultmann the radical demythologizer would agree. The man who wants a more objective proof that Jesus rose from the dead is one who is afraid to take the risk to which Christian faith always calls a man.

There is one other problem that Bultmann has to face. There are those who will say that he has not gotten rid of myth because he is still speaking about an "act of God." He says that Jesus lived a fully human life. He calls for no miraculous intervention of the supernatural in the natural world. But still he insists upon speaking of Jesus as an act of God. Is this not mythical? Is this not still speaking of the transcendent in terms of this world?

Bultmann clarifies why he does not think that it is mythical to speak of an act of God. If an act of God is defined in terms of some event that disrupts nature, then an act of God is a myth. But in the Bible God is often seen as acting through what we would call natural events. In the Old Testament, for example, God is seen as acting through a king who releases the Jews from captivity, although no miracles occur. To Bultmann an act of God always occurs in an event that is completely natural and which can be seen as an act of God only by the man who has the eyes of faith. On the other hand, a myth always attempts to give an objective proof; it tells of a miraculous intervention of supernatural power that would banish all doubts. What distinguishes God's act in Christ from a myth is that we cannot objectively prove that God was acting in Christ. An act of God does not force us to believe as the myth attempts to do, but rather it invites us to have faith.

Bultmann can be described as a radical conservative. In dealing with the historicity of the New Testament he is second to none in his radical approach. He refuses to protect the New Testament history from the most radical of doubts. He is willing to grant that a great deal of the language of the New Testament is mythical. We must not blur the nature of Christian faith by trying to get men to believe in miraculous interventions in nature. All of this makes Bultmann an exciting leader for the radical wing of theologians. But just as the radicals are fully captivated, Bultmann suddenly turns upon them with the conservative emphasis that God has acted decisively in Christ to save men. At this point the radicals drop away in disappointment, fearing that Bultmann has gotten cold feet and abandoned his radicalism. On the other hand, the conservative who reads Bultmann cannot really believe that Bultmann means his conservative statements after his radical points have been made. Both conservatives and radicals unite in declaring that Bultmann is inconsistent in holding to both his radical and conservative claims. But Bultmann remains undisturbed. Clinging to the reality of the new life that he has found through the preaching of the risen Christ, he dares to treat all worldly securities with scorn. In Bultmann, at least, radical trends have found themselves at home with a conservative faith.

10

Dietrich Bonhoeffer
and Worldly Christianity

One of the most influential figures in theology today is
Dietrich Bonhoeffer. For about a decade after his
death in 1945 he was remembered chiefly as a martyr,
but for the last decade his thinking has been a major
inspiration to theologians of widely different persua-
sions. It may seem strange that he should have such a
powerful impact upon theologians and young people
today because his style of writing was heavy and obscure. He chose for his major works titles like *Sanc-
torum Communio* and *Act and Being*. These are not
titles that launch best sellers.

To a great extent the influence of Bonhoeffer today
is based on his life. The son of a German psychiatrist,
he was born in 1906. He was active in the ecumenical
life of the worldwide Church. He was one of the first
Germans to detect the evil of Nazism. Because of his
outspoken criticism of Hitler's regime he often had to
work underground. For a time he was in charge of an
illegal seminary. He left Germany for certain periods,
including a time when he was pastor in an English
parish. As the war clouds gathered in 1939 he was
visiting in the United States. His friends urged him to

stay but he felt that he could only cooperate in the postwar rebuilding of Germany if he had been there through the dark years, so he returned home.

The great German theologians of the thirties had to decide how they must act in the face of Nazism. Barth and Tillich were forced to flee. Bultmann managed to keep his teaching post throughout the Nazi era despite tension. Bonhoeffer chose to return to Germany, to become involved in the underground resistance movement, and to join the group that plotted to assassinate Hitler. He was arrested April 5, 1943 and spent two years in prison. Just before the American troops arrived to liberate his area, he was hanged at Flossenbürg on April 9, 1945.

While in prison he won the respect and love of his fellow prisoners and the guards. The latter allowed him to smuggle out letters to his friend Eberhard Bethge. These letters, published as *Prisoner for God*, have been the main source of Bonhoeffer's rise to theological prominence in the last decade. Bonhoeffer died, as he had lived, witnessing to his faith. The guards came to take him to his death just as he was finishing a worship service with his fellow prisoners. He said quietly to a friend, "This is the end. For me the beginning of life."

The reader of *Prisoner for God* is often overcome with embarrassment. He feels like a wiretapper listening in on a private conversation. These are personal letters to a friend, written more as therapy for the writer than as theological treatises. They reveal the anguished heart of a sensitive soul living in a Nazi prison that was threatened daily by Allied bombing raids. Often the letters are a strange mixture of hope and despair. In one letter Bonhoeffer says confidently that he will soon be released and, a few lines later, he requests certain hymns to be sung at his funeral. The letters reveal the nostalgic homesickness of the writer as he thinks of family and friends. Bonhoeffer gave strength and courage to all who met him but in the letters he lifts the veils from a heart that is threatened with fear and doubt. He reports his harsh words to another prisoner who had displayed degrading cowardice and then wrestles with his conscience over what he had said.

Bonhoeffer had some harsh things to say about the loss of privacy in our modern world. He was opposed to making public the inner self of a person. What would he have thought if he had known that the letters in which he poured out the depths of his soul would become a best-selling book? And yet, how much poorer modern theology would be without these letters! Reading them is more spiritually rewarding than the reading of books that are advertised as "devotional." These letters were not meant as theological treatises, yet they have stimulated exciting trends in theology.

A major problem in interpreting Bonhoeffer is deciding what is the significance of his prison letters. Are they a totally new direction or are they to be read in the light of his earlier systematic writings? Some have feared (and others have rejoiced) that Bonhoeffer lost his faith in prison and that his thought had moved away from Christianity. Others argue that, although he did not lose his faith, he did come to see that

Christianity must be totally reconstructed, so that nothing in his earlier writings can throw light on his new theological direction. Still others claim that there is nothing new in the prison letters. In short, scholars today are engaged in what we might call "The Search for the Historical Bonhoeffer."

In a book of this size and nature we cannot attempt to justify or document our particular interpretation, but we must indicate what it is. To this writer it appears that Bonhoeffer was a creative and dynamic thinker who was continually developing his thought. Naturally the time in prison forced him into a serious theological reevaluation. But, instead of any radically new elements in his prison letters, we see in them new emphases on certain facets of his thought.

Those who interpret the prison letters as a radical break with his earlier thought have overlooked the presence of the same themes in his earlier writings. His last major work, never completed, is his *Ethics*. In this book we find most of the themes that we find in the prison letters and they are developed further than the letters could do. But even in his earlier thought, as we see it in the collection of his occasional writings, *No Rusty Swords,* we find the seeds from which much in the prison letters grew.

Bonhoeffer had a great gift for putting his thought into striking phrases. One such phrase is "cheap grace." Bonhoeffer challenged the Protestant churches in general, and his own Lutheran church in particular, with gathering like eagles "round the carcase of cheap grace." Cheap grace promises that, if we believe certain doctrines, our sins will be forgiven without effort on our part. This comforts Christians when they fail to live differently from non-Christians. Cheap grace preaches forgiveness without repentance.

Cheap grace arises from emphasis upon grace as freely given. Bonhoeffer was far too good a Lutheran to deny that, but God's free grace is not cheap. It is costly. It renews and remakes a man's life; his old nature must die. In Luther, Bonhoeffer found a symbol of this. When Luther went into the monastery it was a costly sacrifice by which he hoped to earn his salvation. But in the monastery he learned that God's grace is not for the spiritual athletes and it is not to be purchased. Just as Luther despaired, he found that the hand of God came to him in grace. As Luther grasped it, he found that it was costly grace. Once more he had to forsake all and follow Christ. But this time he had to follow Christ back into the world.

Luther's return to the world was a greater attack upon the evil of the world than his flight from it had been. Instead of being freed from works, Luther found that God's grace had called him to take discipleship more seriously. But, charged Bonhoeffer, Lutherans have forgotten Luther's insight. They have made Christianity nothing more than going to church to be told that they are forgiven. They have forgotten that Christians are called to be disciples. Thus Bonhoeffer entitled his book *The Cost of Discipleship* (1937). After attacking cheap grace, Bonhoeffer turns to the Sermon on the Mount as a study in the meaning of discipleship. His book ends with a look at the Church as the place where the disciple finds the source of strength that enables him to live the costly life of discipleship. Later, in his book, *Life Together,* Bonhoeffer made a more detailed study of the life of the worshiping Church as a community in which is found the power to live as a Christian.

In his prison letters Bonhoeffer sees some dangers in his book *The Cost of Discipleship*. There is no question that it runs the danger of legalism. Still, Bonhoeffer said in prison that he would stand by what he had written. It was a word that the Church had to speak and hear as it lived under Nazism. Hitler did not mind Christians going to Church to hear that they were forgiven but he could not tolerate them when they became Christ's disciples regardless of cost. In prison Bonhoeffer continued to draw strength from much of the worship life he had outlined in *Life Together*. When he spoke of a worldly holiness or worldly Christianity he was continuing to develop his theme of costly discipleship.

Other phrases with which Bonhoeffer stirred men's minds were his affirmations that "the world has come of age" and grown "beyond religion" so that we must present a "religionless Christianity." The theme of religionless man and religionless Christianity had run through Bonhoeffer's thinking for several years. But in prison he saw with a new sense of urgency the problem that this created for the Church. For a long time theologians had developed their defense of Christianity on the assumption that all men are religious. This religious nature of man was the point at which the Christian could begin speaking to men. Theologians tried to demonstrate that the religious aspirations of men find their most adequate fulfill-

ment in Christian faith. This is what Schleiermacher
did when he began with the universal religious feeling
of men and argued from it to the superiority of Christianity.

Bonhoeffer singles out Tillich as an example of
approaching the unbeliever on the assumption that he
is already religious. Tillich argues that all men are
religious because they are ultimately concerned. He
attempts to demonstrate that the God revealed in
Christ is alone worthy of ultimate concern. Bonhoeffer
charges that Tillich attempted to understand the
world better than it understood itself and thus it felt
misunderstood. The problem, as Bonhoeffer came to
see it, is that Tillich fails to see that men are no
longer religious so that any attempt to approach them
through their religion is doomed to fail. What, asks
Bonhoeffer, is the place of God, prayer, Christ, worship, and the Church in the total absence of religion?

When Bonhoeffer asks about the place of God,
prayer, the Church, and the like in the absence of
religion, it sounds strange. Given our common definitions of religion, if we have God, prayer, worship, and
the Church, we have religion. But the word religion
has no universally accepted definition. We need to see
what Bonhoeffer means by "religion" if we are to understand his call for religionless Christianity.

In the first place Bonhoeffer sees religion as divid-
ing life and the world into two spheres, sacred and
secular, or holy and profane. Religion sees certain
men, professions, acts, and books as sacred and the rest
of life as profane. Men and actions dedicated to the
sacred are of higher value than those dedicated to the

profane. Life to the religious man is the scene of tension and conflict between the demands of the sacred and the profane. The more religious a man becomes the more time and energy he gives to the sacred realm and the less he spends on the profane.

Throughout his life Bonhoeffer fought this division into sacred and secular. We have seen that in his analysis of costly discipleship he emphasized that we must serve Christ in the world (i.e. the realm of the profane) and not in the monastery (i.e. the sacred place). As early as 1932 Bonhoeffer wrote that the Church is not meant to be a consecrated sanctuary but "the world, called by God to God." Thus the Church does not retire to a sacred existence but goes forth into the world to bear the presence of God.

In his *Ethics* Bonhoeffer has a passage in which he decries the tendency of the Church to think in terms of "two spheres." When the Church thinks of two spheres, it is tempted to build itself up as a sacred institution so that it becomes simply a "religious society." Instead, argues Bonhoeffer, the Church must be in the world, working for the salvation of the world and reminding men that God loves the world. The task of the Christian is not to lead a pious life (i.e. majoring in the sacred area), but to be a witness to Christ in the world through life and action. The man who dedicates himself to the pious life makes a mockery of God. This is why Luther could say that God would rather hear the curses of the ungodly than the alleluias of the pious. Bonhoeffer sees a "hopeless godlessness" in the Church which, while disobeying God, calls on his name. On the other hand, there is a "hopeful godlessness" in the world which is a protest against the pious godlessness that has corrupted the Church.

When, in the prison letters, Bonhoeffer called for a religionless Christianity, he was not making a sharp break with his past thinking. There is, however, a new emphasis. In the earlier writings his main thought was that the Christian faith itself calls men away from religion. But in prison he became convinced that modern man had outgrown religion so that an appeal to man's religion was no longer an effective point of contact for Christianity. Christianity's last excuse for advocating religion had disappeared.

Religion has disappeared, believes Bonhoeffer, because man has "come of age." Modern man explains all questions and solves all problems without reference to God. It seems, says Bonhoeffer, that God is teaching man that he can live without God. God has allowed himself to be edged out of the world and onto a cross because it is not by his omnipotence that God saves the world but through his weakness in Christ. Thus the world, come of age, has cleared the decks for the God of the Bible. Jesus offers man the opposite of what religious man expects. Religious man assumes that, by turning his back on the world and by giving more time and energy to the sacred, he will be rewarded with happiness and the absence of suffering. But the biblical God calls man to plunge into the godless world and share the sufferings of God.

In the second place, by religion Bonhoeffer means a metaphysical system to explain the world. Man longs to understand and explain his existence. Metaphysics is the means of explanation to which man turns when his ordinary reasoning runs out. This leads to what Bonhoeffer calls "the god of the gaps." That is, where we have no knowledge we say piously that here is where God acts. Primitive man had to use his gods to explain most of his experiences. As man's thinking progressed he found natural explanations for more experiences but still there remained some gaps in his knowledge and here he continued to use God as his explanation. Even today there are Christians who say that no scientist is able to produce life in his laboratory. Therefore, the creation of life can be exlained only as God's action. But the time is coming when the scientists will produce life in their test tubes and another gap will be closed.

The problem with the god of the gaps is that he is increasingly an unemployed god. Science has filled one after another of the gaps. Man, come of age, says Bonhoeffer, no longer needs the hypothesis of God to solve his problems. Religion, in the sense of a metaphysics to round out our explanation and knowledge of the world, has become obsolete. But this is not a serious loss for the man of biblical faith. The biblical God is not to be found in what we do not know but in what we know.

Another aspect of religion for Bonhoeffer is that religion deals with man's inwardness and individuality. The philosopher Whitehead once defined religion as what a man does with his solitariness. Bonhoeffer would agree but whereas Whitehead extolled such religion, Bonhoeffer deplored it. The Old Testament, he argues, has no interest in personal or individual salvation and, properly understood, neither does the New Testament.

The appeal to religion as inwardness corresponds to both the sacred-secular division and the god of the gaps. Man turns to his inner life, away from the world, to find the sacred realm. As man uses God to fill the gaps in his knowledge, so he turns to God as the *deus ex machina* to solve his personal problems when his own efforts run into a dead end. God becomes the cosmic bellhop to bring happiness to man and overcome his inward despair.

When theology builds upon the foundation of man's religious nature it becomes distorted. It must attack man come-of-age and call him back to servile dependence. It must retire to the boundaries of life to find a place for itself. At the boundaries of death, guilt, and despair it finds weakness and failures and exploits them to win men to religion. The religious approach ends up trying to persuade perfectly happy men that they are really unhappy so that they will turn to God to find happiness and strength.

Theologians who base Christianity on religion have turned in recent years to depth psychology and existentialist philosophy as allies. Both of these have analyzed man in terms of his underlying despair and anxious insecurity. Bonhoeffer contemptuously refers to them as "secularized Methodism." Such an approach, he says, can appeal to only a "small number of intellectuals, of degenerates, of people who regard themselves as the most important things in the world and hence like looking after themselves." But the ordinary man is too busy with his work, family, and hobbies to worry about his intellectual despair.

To Bonhoeffer a theological attack upon the adulthood of the world is ignoble, pointless, and unchristian. It is ignoble because it attempts to take advantage of man in his weakness. It gives rise to the "priestly" snuffing around in the sins of men in order to catch them out. It is religious blackmail. Jesus did speak to weak and sinful men and gave them a message of hope, but he never exploited their weaknesses or attempted to make them feel worse than they already felt. He made no attempt to convert the thieves crucified with him until one of them had first approached him. The attack upon adulthood is pointless because, in a world come of age, men cannot be thrust back into their adolescence. It is unchristian because it attempts to force Christ back into a past stage of man's religiousness. It degrades God to the place of a stopgap for man's weakness and a satisfier of man's selfish desires.

For religion, the ideal man is the *Homo-religiosis,* that is, a "saint" in the popular sense of that word: a pious individual who retires into an inner life of prayer away from the tainted atmosphere of the world. From the beginning of his career Bonhoeffer was uncomfortable in the presence of the pious. He preferred the fellowship of unbelievers to those who talked too much about God. God calls us, he argues, not to become saints but to become men. We ought not to try to be more religious than God himself. God was not too proud to become a man and live a human life. The saint cannot be bothered with the pleasures of the world but Bonhoeffer says that this is ingratitude to God for his gifts. It is improper for a man to long for the transcendent when he is in the arms of his wife. The saint has his eyes set on another world; he grows homesick for heaven, as an old hymn puts it. But, argues Bonhoeffer, God has put us into this world and while we are here it is with this world that we are to be concerned.

In prison Bonhoeffer attempted to work out a wordly or religionless expression of the Christian faith. He admitted that the task was more difficult than he had expected. At one point he argued that our present language has lost its power and we have no new language to put into its place. Perhaps all that we can do is to continue a life of prayer to God and service to our fellowmen and wait for the Holy Spirit to give us the words that will again speak with power to the world. Although Bonhoeffer was not given time to complete his thought, we do receive a fairly clear picture of the direction in which he strove to go. This direction may be seen if we compare him with other major theologians. Bishop J.A.T. Robinson's popular book, *Honest to God*, gave the unfortunate impression that Bonhoeffer was quite close to Bultmann and Tillich in his thinking. In fact, Bonhoeffer repudiated both of them.

Bultmann's demythologization is an attempt to meet Bonhoeffer's world come of age. Modern man cannot accept the mythical world picture of the Bible so it must be reinterpreted existentially. Bonhoeffer, however, was not satisfied. He charges that Bultmann is not nearly radical enough. His attempt to get rid of miracles is doomed to fail because God and miracles go together. What we must do is speak of God and miracles in a nonreligious sense. Bultmann, however, remains within the realm of religion as is manifest in his use of Heidegger's existentialism. Bultmann's concern with man's attempt to find authentic life is a modern way of seeking individual salvation which is a mark of religion.

Bonhoeffer criticizes Bultmann for abandoning miracles but he criticizes Barth for trying to keep all of the miracles. Bonhoeffer argues that the Bible itself forces us to see that some miracles are more important than others. Thus the resurrection of Christ holds a unique place. Against Bultmann, Bonhoeffer says, "This mythology (resurrection and so on) is the thing itself. . . ." In the prison letters he tells us that Socrates mastered the art of dying but that Christ overcame death. That is the meaning of Easter. The Resurrection is unlike all myths because the myths promise salvation from out of the world but the Resurrection drives Christians back into the world. Myths arise from the boundary situation; Christ takes hold of man at the heart of his life.

There are those who find Bonhoeffer inconsistent at this point and it is even suggested that if he had lived longer he would have changed his mind. Such critics argue that if Bonhoeffer had taken with full seriousness the world's coming of age he would not have tried to preach the resurrection of Jesus to it. But this overlooks a consistent theme that runs through Bonhoeffer's work, including the prison letters. On the one hand, he is certain that there is no religious escape from the world that has come of age. But Bonhoeffer recognizes that there is a kind of love of the world that is opposed to Christian faith. The wrong love of the world accepts it as it is: Christian love goes to the world to redeem it. Bonhoeffer charges that Bultmann fell into the error of liberal theology. Both Bultmann and the liberals allowed modern man to become a new law that assigned to Christ his place in the world. Christ came to reconcile the world. This shows, for Bonhoeffer, that the world needs salvation and that it cannot save itself. The Christian who loves the world must not, therefore, capitulate to it for then he would have nothing to bring to it. If one limits Christian belief to what modern man can accept at any particular moment, then Christian faith will lose its saving power.

Bonhoeffer's opposition to Tillich has been mentioned. For Bonhoeffer, Tillich begins with the false premise that man is religious by nature so that we can win him to Christ by appealing to his religion. Furthermore, Tillich appeals to the ultimate issues of life where man meets God at the boundaries and is ultimately concerned. It is at the point of doubt where one finds the "courage to be." To Bonhoeffer all of this is another religious appeal to man's weakness.

Bonhoeffer's relationship to Barth is more complex. Bonhoeffer was more deeply influenced by Barth than by any other theologian. In his prison letters he recalls that Barth was the first theologian to produce a drastic criticism of religion. Barth's definition of religion is somewhat different from Bonhoeffer's. Barth defines religion as man's search for God whereas Christian faith is man's response to God's search for man. But Barth and Bonhoeffer agree that Christianity is not an inward seeking to solve one's problems nor a retreat into some sacred realm. Both agree that the place for the Christian is in the world, living as a disciple of Christ.

Despite his agreement with Barth, Bonhoeffer criticizes him in his prison letters. He charges that Barth met the crisis of the world come of age with a "positivism of revelation." This phrase, which Bonhoeffer fails to explain, is obscure. The basic problem that he seems to see in Barth is that he presented revelation on a "take it or leave it" basis. Barth does not strive sufficiently to interpret the message of revelation for men today. Despite his commendable attack upon religion, Bonhoeffer feels that Barth did not advance the attempt to think through a nonreligious interpretation of the Gospel.

How did Bonhoeffer picture religionless Christianity? Certainly he did not mean that men should leave the Church or quit praying and worshiping. But throughout his life he attacked the idea that there are any spheres of life that do not belong to Christ. Christ cannot be shut up in the sacred society of the Church. As we must find God in our knowledge and in our strength, so we must serve Christ as Lord in the marketplace and the scientist's laboratory. The Bible does not justify giving a special preference to man's inner life as though that were the location of his sacred talents. It sees man as a totality and it is man as a whole who is claimed by God. Thus the place for the Church is not on the borders of life but at the center of the village.

In his *Ethics* Bonhoeffer has a passage that throws considerable light on religionless Christianity. He takes as his foil the popular ethics of Dilschneider who argues that Christian ethics is concerned with the Christian economist or statesman but has nothing to say about economics or politics. (The reader will see the similarity between Dilschneider's argument and the view, often expressed in America, that the duty of the Church is to save souls and deal with spiritual matters without getting involved in political or social problems.) Bonhoeffer quickly puts his finger on the crucial question. Is the Church limited to ministering to the unfortunate ones who have been crushed by the wheels of social institutions or does the Church have a duty to prevent their being crushed?

For Bonhoeffer, the question must be answered in terms of Christ's lordship. This means that there is nothing that stands outside of relationship to Christ. The Church is the place where Jesus Christ is known and loved and therefore the Church has a responsibility for the whole world which God loves. It is only through Christ that everything, from man to the State and economy, has its proper essence. This is not to say that we should strive for a "Christian" state or economy but we must seek a state and an economy that is rightly ordered for the sake of Christ. Christ, as the Lord, comes to these institutions, not as a stranger but to his own. Under the dominion of Christ they find their true character. Christians ought not to strive to bring social institutions under the control of a priesthood nor is it their goal to convert a few key leaders. Instead, they seek to free the institutions to be truly worldly. By working within the world's institutions for justice, the Christian enables Christ's lordship to be made manifest through them. Just as the Christian is to strive to be a true man and not a saint, so the State ought to be a true State and not a "religious society."

This approach to the world through the lordship of Christ has some interesting consequences. Bonhoeffer notes that Christianity has some hopeful things to say to sinners but we still must not forget that God is also the God of the good. Sentimental versions of Christianity have so emphasized the message to sinners that they have nothing to say to the good. But in times like ours, says Bonhoeffer, we need to take another look at the good—those who labor for justice, who fight inhumanity wherever they find it. They too are sinners but their sin is not their goodness, it is their separation from the Lord of their being. In approaching them we must not try to make them think that their good deeds are filthy rags, no better than the deeds of harlots or Nazis. We must not strive to catch them in "slips" but rather we must lead them to see how their good deeds point to Christ.

We cannot help but be amazed at the vision that Bonhoeffer caught in prison. If ever there was a place where we might expect a man to retire into his inner life to find God at the point of his weakness, we would assume that it would be a Nazi prison that was a target for Allied bombers. And yet this is the place from whence Bonhoeffer called the Church to quit bemoaning man's knowledge and strength and to cease trying to exploit man's weakness. A few years ago a popular religious leader was quoted in the newspapers as saying that too many Americans were taking sleeping pills instead of turning to God. Bonhoeffer would not have been too concerned about this. What he would have criticized is that too many religious leaders are offering God as a substitute for sleeping pills.

How would Bonhoeffer have developed his thought had more time been given to him? We cannot answer with certainty but a few directions seem likely. He once referred to God as being not on the boundaries of life but as "the Beyond in the midst of life." This, of course, is a reaffirmation of the traditional Christian view that God is both immanent and transcendent. God is to be found in what we know, not in what we do not know. When we try to find God in what we do not know, the gaps, we are thinking of God on a level with the things that we do know. He is the First Cause, for example. We know what a cause is in normal situations, but we do not know what caused the whole universe. So here, too, there must be a cause, we say, only a bigger and better cause than other causes. But despite our reference to "bigger and better," God has become just another one in a series. He is no longer the "Beyond."

But if God is the Beyond in the midst of life, we confess that God is in the processes that we know, working through them, but working in a dimension different from causes. In normal situations we recognize that there are different dimensions. The detective looks at the dead man and asks, "What was the cause of his death?" This is a question to be answered, in one dimension, by an autopsy. But when the detective asks, "What was the motive behind this death?" he is still referring to the same set of facts in the world but he is looking at them from a different perspective, and the answer to this question involves a different dimension. An autopsy will not locate a motive. God, as the Beyond in our midst, is to be found, not in a few exotic experiences or situations, but as a dimension in the whole of life.

From out of prison Bonhoeffer spoke to tell the world that God and Christian faith cannot henceforth bloom as a hothouse plant, protected from the godless world where man has come of age. The Christian is called by Christ to plunge himself into the life of this world. He is not, says Bonhoeffer, in one of his last letters, to fall into that shallow kind of worldliness of the "enlightened, of the busy, the comfortable or the lascivious." It must be something much more, something in which the "knowledge of death and resurrection is ever present." Man must quit trying to make himself into something special, such as a saint; he must take life in his stride. Only thus can he throw himself into God's arms and participate in his sufferings. Because, said Bonhoeffer, "I discovered and am still discovering up to this present moment that it is only by living completely in this world that one learns to believe."

11

Theological Directions Today

J. Robert Nelson, in a tribute to Emil Brunner, noted that Brunner died only a few months after Paul Tillich. This leads Nelson to say, "And the question keeps nagging us: where are their successors?" Today we look in vain for anyone who appears likely to make a contribution in any way comparable to that made by the theologians at whom we have looked. At the present moment theology cannot be divided into three or four schools led by major thinkers. On the contrary, it seems that theology is becoming atomized into an increasingly baffling number of trends, schools, and moods.

Although theology lacks outstanding leadership today, it has broken into the news again in a way that is comparable to the early days of the fundamentalist-liberal controversy. The layman meets theological issues in all of his news media. Almost annually a new best-selling theological book hits the market. The sale of these books indicates that there is interest in theological issues, although it also indicates the enjoyment the public feels whenever it observes a good fight.

Theology today is agitated and restless with controversy. When I wrote the first edition of this book in

1954 I said that "there is a tendency for theologians to search for a middle ground, and to find agreement apart from the extremes." This tendency grew through the late fifties. It became common to hear neo-orthodox thinkers admitting that they had laid aside too quickly some truths of liberalism while liberals spoke warmly about the needed corrections made by neo-orthodoxy. Conservatives found helpful insights in both of the former groups. Some time early in the sixties all of this began to change. Once again theologians began attacking each other. It is no longer considered cricket for one theologian to attack another as "heretical" but theologians today reject opponents by branding them "irrelevant."

We cannot, in the space that is left, do more than point briefly to some of the major trends in recent theology. It is too early to decide which, if any, of them is the voice of the future and thus worthy of more extensive treatment. It is hoped that the reader will be inspired to follow the new trends for himself.

Behind all of the latest trends in theology there lies a deep concern to come to grips with the realities of our age. (Thus irrelevancy is the worst crime with which to charge a theologian.) The reader of the foregoing chapters will realize that this is by no means new. Is there a single theologian at whom we have looked who did not share this concern? What then is new? There is today a sense that the world is changing more rapidly than ever before and that any theology or church that is to speak to it must be prepared to change rapidly and radically.

The changing patterns of our world are found on many levels. Most obvious is technological change. Not only have we moved into the space age, we have moved into the age of automation and computers. Marshall McLuhan is gaining a wide hearing for his thesis that modern methods of communication are changing the patterns of our thinking even more drastically than was done by the invention of printing. Closely allied with the technological revolution is the knowledge explosion. We are told that our factual knowledge is doubling every ten years. A man who graduated from college ten years ago in almost any field is hopelessly out of date if he has not struggled to keep studying.

Perhaps more significant than the technological and knowledge revolutions is the revolution of "rising expectations." Of course, this is related to the fact that technology has opened new vistas for living. The poor and dispossessed of the world are demanding a fair share of the good things of life. The day is long past when the rich could hope to win praise by passing out charity and "foreign aid" to the less fortunate. Revolutions in imperialistic colonies and riots in racial ghettoes are symptoms of a new life being claimed by the dispossessed.

We hear about the ethical revolution of our time. Naturally the items that make the headlines are questions about a new sexual morality and the use of drugs such as LSD. But it goes much deeper. This ethical revolt is closely associated with a division between the generations. An increasingly number of young people are rejecting the way of life that their parents consider good. Many quote from other times and places to remind us that in every society youth and age have lived in tension. Is there something different today? If Marshall McLuhan is correct, the college youth of today has been brought up in a drastically different intellectual environment from that of his parents. He has a different set of values. Beards, Beatniks, and Beatles symbolize a way of life that those over forty are not expected to understand.

In addition to all of this the theologian recognizes that Christendom is past. That is, we no longer live in a culture in which the majority of people accept Christian values. As the non-Christian countries win the battle of the cradle, Christians become a shrinking minority. Countries that once seemed safely Protestant are now being reminded by battles over Christmas pageants and prayers in the schools that they are pluralistic societies where no religion or creed can claim preference. Society has become secular in the sense that it is no longer controlled by ecclesiastical groups.

In a world of change Christians are haunted by the need to speak to their times. At the same time many believe that the Church has become simply a force for preserving the past; that it is centered on its own welfare and is unwilling to risk its life to serve the strange new world. As we take our quick glance at the theological currents of today, we must keep this environment in mind.

One of the dominant themes in modern theology is expressed by the slogan "worldly" or "secular" Christianity. These terms, inspired by Bonhoeffer, describe Christians who feel called to enter into social and political spheres to serve God and man. The word "secularism" has had an interesting history in theology. In 1928, at the Jerusalem meeting of the International Missionary Council, war was declared on secularism by an American liberal, Rufus Jones, who had spent his life fighting for a better world. He declared that the great rival of Christianity is no longer Buddhism, Islam, or any of the other religions, but secularism. For Jones, secularism meant an ordering of life without reference to God or spiritual reality. The secularist may or may not pay lip service to God but he lives as though there were no God. For two or three decades Jones' interpretation formed a battle slogan for the ecumenical movement. For example, in 1937 the Oxford conference met under the shadow of Nazism. To most delegates Nazism seemed to be the logical conclusion of secularism. Having ignored God, man fell to worshiping his State.

In 1954, Edwin Aubrey, another American liberal, published a book with the title *Secularism a Myth*. The book has been forgotten because it was published about twelve years too soon. It came at a time when no theologian was ready to listen to a good word for secularism. Aubrey's thesis was that the term had become a myth that theologians used to describe everything that they did not like. He listed some twenty-seven items that were brushed aside under the term secularism. Aubrey called on theology to quit firing broadsides at an indefinite target and to analyze carefully the contributions of the modern world in terms of both strengths and weaknesses.

Under the influence of Bonhoeffer the theological climate changed. With startling rapidity secular became a good word and theologians began to boast, "I am more secular than thou." How did such a change occur? In part it resulted from a new definition of the term. Harvey Cox, one of the most popular advocates of secularity, draws a distinction between "secularism," which he repudiates, and "secularization," which he embraces. By secularization, Cox means the historical process, which he believes is irreversible, whereby societies are delivered from ecclesiastical control and closed metaphysical views. It frees man from the idea that he is bound by fate or limited by sacred areas of life into which he dare not enter. The center of interest is this world and not some supernatural realm. On the other hand, for Cox, secularism is an ideology which brings a new closed world view and which functions very much like a new religion.

For Cox, the cornerstone of modern secularization is found in the Bible itself. The biblical doctrine of creation "disenchanted" nature. That is, by affirming that the world is created by God, it showed that the world is not sacred, only God is. Thus the world can be studied by science and manipulated by man. Secondly, the Exodus of the Jews from Egypt "desacralized" politics. When the Jews revolted against the "duly constituted monarch" they declared that no government is sacred or above criticism. Henceforth throughout Jewish history the prophets opposed their kings in God's name. No longer could any government claim unquestioning obedience. Finally, at Sinai values were "deconsecrated." When God forbade idolatry he showed man that the values built by a culture are never absolute or worthy of ultimate allegiance.

There is another dimension to Cox's secularity. Although the theoretical basis of secularization was laid in the Bible, it was not until the rise of the modern city that it could be fully expressed. Man had lived through the time of the tribe and the town. But today the majority of men live in the city and all are influenced by the thinking of the city. It is popular to deplore the city because it makes for impersonal life. But Cox applauds the fact that city dwelling has freed man. In the tribe and the town men lived under the continual observance of their neighbors and they were not free to choose friends. In the city we have satisfying but passing relations with most people. We ignore the man next door and are ignored by him. This leaves us free to live as we desire and to choose the friends that we want.

Life in the city is mobile (even as the biblical Jews were a nomadic people) and men are not chained to the place, job, or social condition which they inherit. In the city talents and knowledge can be mobilized for an organized attack upon man's problems; new ways of life can be achieved through human effort.

Cox is convinced that the Church must cease to bewail or oppose secularization. Since the Bible is behind it, the Church should welcome it. Instead of attempting to promote a way of life that was adequate to the time of the tribe and town, the Church must be God's *avant-garde* in the city. The Church is not primarily an institution; it is a people, the people who are prepared "to go where the action is" to work for a better world.

Cox attempts, like Bonhoeffer, to speak of God in a secular way. He repudiates Tillich's metaphysical lan-

guage as an outworn remnant of another age. Bultmann's demythologization has only translated the
Bible into the metaphysics of yesterday. Cox argues
that in a secular age we must not speak metaphysically
of God; we must speak of him in political analogies.
In the time of the town persons met each other in I-
thou relations and thus theology thought of God in
terms of I-thou. In the city a new type of relationship
is developing. It is not I-thou but neither is it I-it; it is
a relationship of alongsidedness which might be called
I-you. It describes our satisfying relationship with a
fellow team member. Contemporary man must meet
God as "you." In Jesus God entered into teamwork
with man. Instead of being fascinated with God himself, we must be more concerned with the work that
we do with God. Like Bonhoeffer before him, Cox
confesses that the task of speaking of God in a secular
way is extremely difficult. But he sees no other hope
for theology.

Cox is not the only theologian of secularity today.
Others would not agree with all of his points. Few are
as optimistic as is Cox about the values of the modern
city. Secular theologians do agree that the problems of
this world should be a chief concern for the Christian.
They deplore the many ways in which the Church has
rationalized its failures to confront social and political
evils. We shall look at just one other trend of the
secular theologians—the concern to find new church
forms to serve the world.

Colin Williams has written several books criticizing
the preoccupation of the modern Church with the
local congregation based on residence. Williams does

not claim that such congregations are totally obsolete, but he believes that they are no longer capable of doing many of the things that the Church must do today. By making the local congregation the key structure of the Church, we have divided the Church along the same lines of social, economic, and racial segregation as the communities in which we live. We have divided the Church from work, for people no longer live where they work. Furthermore, the task of maintaining the local parish often monopolizes the time of laymen to the point where they see no call to Christian service outside of the affairs of the congregation.

In another age the local congregation was uniquely geared to meet the problems of the world. In a town everyone knew who were the alcoholics and who were in economic distress. The local congregation might or might not have fulfilled its obligations to such people but at least it had the organization to do so. But in today's city the alcoholics and other outcasts form sub-groups that fall out of sight. The slums are far from suburban congregations and Christian consciences are not stirred by seeing poverty at first hand. To meet the needs of persons in the city, says Williams, the Church must develop new structures that can go where the people are.

There is another theological group that makes use of the term "secular," but which is to be distinguished from secular theology as we see it in Cox or Williams. This group is the "God is dead" theologians. Actually, at the time of writing, this is a group made up of two members, Thomas Altizer and William Hamilton. Although wits have commented that the God-is-dead theologians could hold a convention in a telephone booth, these men have created a widespread stir.

The term "God is dead" was originally coined by the philosopher Frederich Nietzsche. It has been used frequently by theologians to describe the fact that for many in our age God seems to be unreal and thus is dead. Gabriel Vahanian brought the term to prominence in his book, *God is Dead,* which appeared in 1957. Vahanian argues that today atheism is not simply a theory which a few thinkers teach; it is a way of life lived by the masses. When he wrote his book Vahanian was aware that there was a revival of religion. But this confirmed his thesis. What was being revived was a religiosity which identified God with man's peace of mind and economic welfare. Nothing could better prove the death of God than the way in which this religiosity lightly used God's name. Vahanian does not believe, however, that God is in fact dead. The living God of biblical faith can be ignored but not killed. And so Vahanian calls Christians to smash the idols worshiped in our time so that the living God might be heard again. The God-is-dead theologians begin from the same view of our culture but draw a different conclusion than Vahanian did. In some real sense they want to say that God is dead.

Altizer is difficult to understand because he speaks in exaggerated and poetic terms. Central to his thinking is the idea that opposites turn out to be identical with each other. Thus he can say enthusiastically, "God is dead, thank God!" and expect us to take both phrases with equal seriousness. He insists that the Christian must accept his own age and think in its terms and yet he finds his chief inspiration in such long-dead thinkers as the philosopher G. W. F. Hegel and the poet William Blake. He can say that God died in Christ, God died in the nineteenth century, God died in the twentieth century, God dies again every time a Christian loves his neighbor, and still he tells us that we must will the death of God. It begins to look as though it takes Altizer's God as long to die as the hero of an Italian opera who rises several times from his deathbed to sing another aria.

Perhaps the best place to start with Altizer is with his emphasis upon Philippians 2:6–8, where we read that Christ, who was in the form of God, "emptied himself, taking the form of a servant . . . and became obedient unto death." For Altizer this means that the transcendent, primordial God actually died in Christ in order that he might enter fully into history. The Church tried to put him back up in heaven through its doctrine of Christ's Resurrection and Ascension. This is one reason why all traditional Christian thought must be repudiated. But the death of God was not completed in Jesus; it expresses a continuing process whereby the Spirit embodies itself in the flesh. With the progressive movement of the Word or Spirit into the flesh of history, a new age is breaking. This age is particularly close to realization in the United States as the poet Blake forecast it would be.

The man who comes to Altizer with hopes of finding a truly atheistic theologian will be disappointed. God's death does not mean that God is no more; it means that he is becoming fully immanent within the world and history. One newspaper reporter commented wryly that had a news bulletin originated in Atlanta (where Altizer teaches) announcing that a theologian said "God is immanent," instead of saying "God is dead," then the bulletin never would have left Atlanta.

William Hamilton is quite different from Altizer. In 1961, Hamilton's book *The New Essence of Christianity* won a modest hearing. In it Hamilton expressed his belief that theology must become humble and fragmentary. The theologian dare not claim to have the knowledge that could develop a systematic description of the whole of life. He needs to dispense with excess baggage and travel light. He must pare away the items to be believed until he reaches the core where he can claim knowledge and this must be proclaimed with passion. The greatest problem faced by faith is suffering and it must be faced honestly. To meet this problem Hamilton turns again to the suffering of Jesus. In Jesus we find God lowly, in the world, serving others. In Jesus' presence we find that we must speak of God himself as suffering. Today's Christian must be a rebel against God because only when we have rebelled against the "father-image" God can we serve the limited and suffering God. In such a spirit the Christian can still live in a suffering world and find a strange enjoyment of life.

In 1964, an article by Hamilton, "Thursday's Child," appeared. It is a description of today's theologian and, though written in the third person, it is generally interpreted as autobiographical. It describes today's theologian as a man who has lost faith in God without being cast into despair. He lives without faith or hope but still clings to love. He seldom reads theological books unless he gets a free copy to review. He does not go to church. He writes letters or articles but not books. He lives in two worlds. Among his churchly friends he adopts a pious attitude but among his secular friends he adopts a worldly attitude. The theologian is waiting; perhaps he will find a new faith but he is not unduly worried about it. For the moment there are tasks to be done, such as the battle for Civil Rights. With Bonhoeffer, therefore, the theologian confesses that traditional theological language is powerless and he can only live in prayer and doing right by his fellowmen.

In later articles Hamilton's position moved away from the idea of waiting. There is no God for whom to wait and there is no more mention of prayer. The Reformation, says Hamilton, has meant three things to twentieth century theology. Liberalism rediscovered Luther as the autonomous individual who followed his conscience against the authoritarian power. Neo-orthodoxy rediscovered the righteous God and Luther's emphasis upon justification through faith. The God-is-dead theology has rediscovered Luther's movement from the cloister to the world.

For Hamilton the cloister symbolizes religion. He defines religion not simply as certain pious or churchly activities but as the view of God as the "problem solver." Religion believes that there are certain needs of man that only God can meet or fulfill. Hamilton asserts that "There is no God-shaped blank within man" waiting to be filled. The world to which the God-is-dead theologian turns is precisely the middle-class world of technology, sex, and the city which so much sophisticated literature and theology have deplored. Today a great many people long to enjoy some of the fruits of middle-class life so that they too can afford to disparage its values.

For Hamilton, the death of God describes an event that many have experienced in our time. Once, for these persons, God was real and language about him was relevant. But something happened and God is no longer real to them. There is some sense of loss but it is not as great as they would have thought. They find that living without God in the world has its own appeal.

The God-is-dead theologian is without God but he is not without Jesus. He is seeking to find Jesus in the world where he is concealed in the battles for justice, beauty, clarity, and order. We find Jesus inasmuch as we love our neighbor. Furthermore, we are to become Jesus in and to the world. When Jesus was asked, "Who is my neighbor?" he told the parable of the Good Samaritan which said, "Don't look for thy neighbor, be one." This is the task of the Christian today.

In 1966, Hamilton published an article entitled "The New Optimism." He argued that a major reason for the decline of neo-orthodoxy is that it was pessimistic about man and the world. Now America has moved beyond pessimism to optimism. He symbolizes this by taking one day, January 4, 1965. On that day T. S. Eliot died. Eliot had described our age as one of the "hollow men" that was to end with a whimper and not a bang. He was the poet of pessimism, much beloved by some of the neo-orthodox. And on that same day Lyndon Johnson delivered his State of the Union message which promised a new day in Civil Rights and the War on Poverty.

Hamilton finds evidence for the new optimism in many places. Saul Bellow, the novelist, rejects existentialism and his hero Herzog commits the post-pessimistic act of deciding not to go mad. Social scientists today believe that technology offers opportunities for overcoming human problems. Art forms are beginning to celebrate the joy of life, as, for example, the delightful Beatles' movie, *A Hard Day's Night*. The Civil Rights movement is winning new battles and singing its faith that "We Shall Overcome." Hamilton emphasizes that this optimism is not an optimism about what God's grace can do, but about what man himself can do to solve his problems.

Hamilton has said that in today's fast-changing world an article is often out of date before it can be published. His article on optimism illustrates his point. By the time it appeared it seemed strangely anachronistic. In 1966, the Vietnam conflict appeared more desperate and hopeless than had been imagined. The War on Poverty was stymied by lack of funds. The Civil Rights movement was atomized into conflicting groups, and laws which had been passed were proving less effective than had been hoped. Riots in the ghettoes were eloquent expressions of frustration at the meager gains in Civil Rights.

Also in 1966, there appeared a book by William Stringfellow, a lawyer with a deep theological interest.

His book, *Dissenter in a Great Society,* illustrates the opposite of Hamilton's position. Having lived several years in the Harlem slums, Stringfellow launches a bitter attack upon the failure of the Great Society to better the lot of the slum dweller. He pictures the nation moving toward a time of increasing violence, burdened with the Vietnam war abroad and torn by racial conflict at home. Stringfellow is no less concerned with taking Christ into the world than Hamilton. In fact, he has lived his life as a Christ to his neighbors in the slums. But, because he has been in the front lines of the War on Poverty and racial discrimination, he knows how limited have been the victories. He too ends his book with optimism, but it is the optimism of a Christian faith which knows that, in Christ, death has been defeated. Christ's death and resurrection are what call us into the world to serve and they alone are the basis for hope. American theology is going to have some interesting debates on the themes represented by Hamilton and Stringfellow.

Paul Van Buren is a theologian who has been linked with the God-is-dead theology both by the news media and by William Hamilton. Van Buren, however, does not consider himself a member of any movement, and he considers it rather nonsensical to say that God is dead. Thus he represents still another option in theology today.

Like many theologians in the last decade, Van Buren turns away from theology's concern with existentialist theology to an alliance with analytical philosophy, which is the dominant philosophy in English-speaking countries. The aim of his book *The Secular Meaning of the Gospel* is to reinterpret Christian faith for man in a secular age. His first concern is not to convert unbelievers but to work out the problem of the man who is both Christian and secular.

To Van Buren secularism means modern man's reaction against idealist philosophy and his emphasis upon empirical methods of knowing. Van Buren finds such secularism illustrated by early forms of analytical philosophy which affirm that the only statements about matters of fact that are meaningful are those which can be verified by empirical means.

Van Buren attempts to describe Christianity in harmony with the biblical message and secularism. The term God is without meaning to secular man so it is necessary to express Christianity without references to God. The New Testament solves all questions about God by referring to Jesus. He who has seen Jesus "has seen the Father" (John 14:9). Since Jesus is an historical figure, secular man can make meaningful statements about him. In Jesus, the first disciples met one who was strangely free to live a life of love for others. After his death the disciples found that the freedom of Jesus had become "contagious" and they were free to love. Down through history the Christian Church has found that the "contagion" continued to operate in the lives of Christians. The meaning of Christ's resurrection is that his freedom to love is contagious. Secular man cannot believe that a man rose from the dead but he can recognize the empirical phenomenon of contagious love.

Van Buren's thought is a fascinating attempt to be

purely secular while remaining loyal to the Gospel. Christ retains a central place in Van Buren's thought and his analogy of contagious love is an attempt to describe in empirical terms what traditional theology has called grace.

In recent years the doctrine of God has moved to the center of theological concern and a host of books have appeared on this subject. This was probably inevitable. Analytical philosophy raised the question whether language about God could be meaningful. The various theologies of the secular asked if we could speak about God in a secular way. The God-is-dead theology raised the question of whether God is real or not.

Although the question of God is of central concern, there is at present no unanimity on how we should speak about him. Bishop Robinson, in his popular book, *Honest to God*, pointed out the problems of thinking about God "up there" and suggested we think of God as being in the depths of life, the Ground of our being. We have seen something of this in Tillich's approach. But others doubted that metaphysical concepts like Ground of Being are any more congenial to modern man than concepts of God "out there."

One group of theologians has tried to reestablish the doctrine of God by rehabilitating the philosophy of A. N. Whitehead. In this group we find a revival of natural theology in the liberal tradition. Most of the members of this school of thought seem to have been associated with the University of Chicago where the philosopher Charles Hartshorne preserved the thinking of Whitehead for several years. This group of theologians is convinced that, to answer the God-is-dead theology, we must demonstrate the objective reality of God by a rational metaphysics. Whitehead seems to them a good beginning.

John Cobb, Jr. argues that man intuitively looks for an explanation for the order in the world. Whitehead found this explanation in his God who is the "principle of Concretion" which brings the actual into being from out of the manifold possibilities. Cobb believes that Christianity must be able to speak about God in some such fashion. It will not do to identify God with some vague "depths" of human existence. Christian belief is justified only if we can speak about God as a reality apart from ourselves but related to us.

There are a number of reasons why a natural theology based on Whitehead appeals to some. Whitehead takes with full seriousness the scientific disciplines. His God is not like the God of traditional metaphysics, a static or perfect Being, but is process. He is becoming so that he has something in common with the living God of biblical faith. But critics argue that Whitehead's philosophy is outdated and they doubt that Whitehead's God can be identified with the God of Christian faith.

Daniel Jenkins, a British theologian, would agree with Cobb that Christian belief depends upon belief in God as a reality apart from ourselves. But his method of showing the reasonableness of belief in God is quite different. Jenkins notes that the term "reason" has a double connotation. In the first place, it is a tool of logic whereby men can sort out arguments and arrive at truth. As such it is, like all tools, neutral. But reasoning is always done by a person who is more than just a mind. Thus reason becomes a means by which man tries to exalt himself. It is ever in danger of becoming rationalization. The closer we come to the center of our life, the more compelling are the temptations to rationalize. The question of God is not a question like the existence of a far-off planet so that it can be studied objectively by natural theology. It is a question that must be answered by the whole direction and commitment of our lives.

For Jenkins, the primary evidence for God is the Bible in general and Christ in particular. For Christians the question of belief in God turns on the question, "What think ye of Christ?" The Bible claims to have a revelation of God. The task of demonstrating the truth of this claim is that of demonstrating that the perspective of the Bible is a more adequate understanding of life than any alternative. Thus Jenkins develops his case by a negative attack upon opposing points of view and a positive demonstration of the adequacy of the Christian frame of reference to illuminate life.

David Jenkins, another British theologian, takes an approach somewhat different from Daniel Jenkins. In a brilliant little book, *Guide to the Debate About God,* he outlines the history of how we have come to the current debate about God. He reminds us that this debate has been going on for some centuries and that the current theories are not as new as some pretend.

David Jenkins says that the real problem is not "Does God exist?" but "What is knowledge?" It is useless to debate with a man who defines knowledge to exclude knowledge of God. It is easy to make the mistake of supposing that the answer to the question of how men think at present is also the answer to the question of what there is to think about. While many today are striving to express the Christian faith within the frame of reference of secular men, Jenkins calls us to reexamine this frame of reference.

The new factor in the debate about God today as compared with the debate in the ancient world is the appearance of science. Jenkins does not see that the findings of science have brought any serious obstacles to belief in God. But with science there has come the conviction that if something is not knowable by science, it does not exist or is not real. Jenkins does not deny that science is the only way to gain knowledge in certain areas. He has no desire to reopen the discreditable debate in which theological arguments were used against scientific theories such as evolution. But he does ask whether the methods of science are capable of knowing everything that can be known. Several years ago E. T. Ramsdell made the same point when he said that although a man may know what he can scientifically verify, he cannot know that what is scientifically unverifiable is insignificant; he can only believe that this is so. Science, affirms Jenkins, is the means whereby men gain knowledge about things in the universe. But God is not a thing. It would be irrational to suppose that we could demonstrate God's existence by the methods that we use to demonstrate the existence of anything else because God is unlike anything else. If we are to think of God at all we must be prepared to think differently from the way we think about things.

If God is, he must make himself known. We must be open to his revelation when and where it comes. The believer must be humble because he never has a demonstration of God whereby he can beat unbelievers over the head to make them believe. Furthermore, Jenkins agrees with Bonhoeffer that God reveals himself in his service to the world and thus the Christian must witness to God through his service in the world. To show others that we have knowledge of God we must live with them in the world, drawing strength from membership in the people of God with its life of worship and commitment. We must be able to show from whence comes our claim to knowledge and what is its nature.

This brief summary of contemporary theological thought will give the reader some idea of the diversity of opinions today. Some call us to be more worldly and secular, others call us to question the presuppositions of secularism. Some say that God is dead and others are working toward a new understanding of God. If we had more space we could point up many other trends. For example, certain followers of Bultmann have revolted against their leader by launching a "New Search for the Historical Jesus." Hoping to overcome the limitations of the nineteenth century search, these men have produced several new "lives" in recent years. Other followers of Bultmann have attempted to develop a "new hermeneutics." Hermeneutics is the means of interpreting a text and these men are wrestling with the problem of interpreting the Bible for man in the twentieth century. Heinrich Ott, who occupies the chair at Basle which Barth occupied until his retirement, is attempting to bring about a synthesis between the theologies of Barth and Bultmann with the help of the later philosophy of Heidegger.

Finally, we must note a most important activity in contemporary Protestant theology—the conversation with Roman Catholic theology. As yet this conversation has not issued in a particular theological viewpoint, but it has thrown new light on all theological concerns. On the one hand, we have men who have written powerful cases for Protestant theology—for example, Robert McAfee Brown—who are finding new theological inspiration through conversation with Catholic scholars. On the other hand, we have Roman Catholic scholars finding surprising agreements with Protestants. Hans Küng has written a book on Barth's doctrine of Justification and has found it in essential harmony with the Roman Catholic position when appropriate allowance is made for the different terminologies used. Without any doubt this interfaith conversation will have a decisive influence on tomorrow's theology.

The reader of this chapter may be struck by the parallels between many thinkers described here and the thought described in our chapter on "The Threat to Orthodoxy." It is also quite evident that many of the themes of liberal theology are reappearing in a somewhat different form. Kenneth Hamilton, a Canadian theologian, has argued that today's theologians who pride themselves on bringing about a theological revolution are, in fact, returning to positions that have been with us for at least two centuries.

There are two ways of interpreting this tendency of theology to return to the past. Many of those who are leading this return claim that from the last century come questions that have not been answered and which neo-orthodoxy bypassed. On the other hand, in a recent book James Smart deplores the fact that those who are calling us today to "go beyond" Barth and Bultmann are, in fact, going backward to a former age and have overlooked the theological gains made in our century. There is probably truth in both of these interpretations. The future theological discussions may reveal which is the more true.

12

Conclusion

The wide varieties of theological thought which we have surveyed may seem deplorable to the reader. Perhaps he has the feeling of being lost in a maze of conflicting ideas. He may feel as many voters feel on the eve of an election: he has listened to the conflicting parties present their views and now he is completely confused about how to vote. And yet, that is the essence of democracy. If there were only one totalitarian party he would not have to choose. I believe that the same principle holds for theology. If there were no theological differences we would have totalitarian religion. Protestantism may well count its differences as its glory, not its shame. Of course, where the differences lead to intolerance and bitterness, we need to repent. But even then we repent not for our difference in views but for our failure to love one another in our differences.

There is a further similarity to the political scene. In an election campaign one hears little about the great realm of ideas which two political parties hold in common. The purpose of the campaign is to bring out differences. If the parties were face to face with a totally alien philosophy, the area of agreement would become apparent. In times of crisis a bipartisan for-

eign policy emerges. This book is something like a
political campaign in that it has not pictured Christians over against their anti-Christian foes. If it had
done that, it would have dwelt on large areas of agreement. Rather it has pictured Christians thinking out
the meaning of their faith along with their fellow
Christians, and we have tried to bring out their dis-
tinctive positions. Actually the representatives of the
various schools of thought that we have described are
to be found working together in our various denominations and in the ecumenical movement of the
Church.

Differences of thought will always be perturbing to
the man who believes that he must have the absolute
truth as it is revealed by God. If one believes that he
has such truth he must believe that all who disagree
with him are not only wrong, they are opposed to
God.

But if we take the position that human truth is
always finite, we must welcome difference. If we believe that infallibility is never attained in human
affairs, we must welcome diversity of thought as a
needed corrective of our own limitations.

I do not wish to be misunderstood here. I am not
advocating that sloppy idea of tolerance that is popular today. You know the kind; it says, "One man's
religious belief is as good as that of any other." Carried to its logical conclusion, this means that Protestantism, Catholicism, Hinduism, Communism, and
Father Divine-ism are all equally true. There is nothing to choose between them. If all religious opinions
are of equal value, it can only mean that none of them

is of any value. It means that we can know nothing about religion.

If we are going to think at all we must assume that we can come to conclusions and that some conclusions will have more to be said for them than others. The fact that we cannot achieve final and absolute truth does not mean that we cannot know some truth. Where would we be in science and politics if we insisted that because we do not know everything, we must suppose that we know nothing and that one idea is as good as another?

If we believe that some truth, but not infallible truth, can be achieved, we will find in the debates of theology a healthy road to truth. We can find that our own position is strengthened by the criticism it receives from other positions. We may be led to abandon ideas that we come to see as false when they are under attack, or we may see a greater truth in them when we see how well they stand up under criticism. We must never forget that we can learn much from positions which, on the whole, we consider to be basically wrong. We can take it almost for granted that no position can hold the allegiance of sincere men if it has no truth whatsoever in it. As Reinhold Niebuhr says, many a truth has ridden into history on the back of an error. Lastly, we must remember that true tolerance does not ignore the difference between conflicting views. It says that it will continue to respect and listen to a man even when he is believed to be wrong. True tolerance recognizes that a man has the right to be wrong and that even when he is most wrong he may have a truth that is needed. A meaningful and creative discussion can be carried out in this spirit alone.

Today it is widely accepted in theological circles that all of man's attempts to speak about God are finite and human efforts to point to a reality that transcends all human expressions. One reason that Catholics and Protestants are entering into a real conversation is that theologians on both sides are taking a more humble view of their abilities than often has been the case in the past. Even where the theologian believes that God has revealed himself infallibly in the Bible or in the Church, he is ready to concede that we do not have infallible understanding of the infallible revelation. Therefore we must listen to the one who disagrees with us because he may have precisely that element of truth which we lack.

A striking development of our century is that theological differences no longer follow denominational lines. Practically all of our major denominations have representatives of most of the positions that we have met in this book. In a particular denomination we may be somewhat more likely to find a particular type of theology, but in every case there are exceptions. Theologically speaking, a Christian often finds himself closer to individuals in another denomination than to many members of his own. The fundamentalist-modernist controversy split denominations (and even congregations) down the middle, and the diversity within denominations has continued. This fact has helped to make the ecumenical movement of this century possible and it also has been stimulated by the ecumenical movement.

This book does not pretend to have been a complete or adequate treatment of modern Protestant theology. Its primary purpose is to stimulate the layman to read further and think more deeply about theological questions. It is meant to be the first step in a journey that will be fruitful and rewarding to the man who chooses to go further.

Suggestions for Further Reading

PROTESTANT THEOLOGY

Brown, Robert M., *The Spirit of Protestantism*. Oxford University Press, 1961.

Edwards, David L., ed., *The Honest to God Debate*. The Westminster Press, 1963.

Ferré, Nels, *Know Your Faith*. Harper & Brothers, 1959.

——— *A Theology for Christian Education*. The Westminster Press, 1967.

Herzog, Frederick, *Understanding God*. Charles Scribner's Sons, 1966.

Jenkins, David E., *Guide to the Debate about God*. The Westminster Press, 1966.

Marty, Martin, and Peerman, Dean, eds., *New Theology*. Vols. 1-4. The Macmillan Company, 1964, 1965, 1966, 1967.

Robinson, John A. T., *Honest to God*. The Westminster Press, 1963.

Schilling, Sylvester P., *Contemporary Continental Theologians*. Abingdon Press, 1966.

Watson, Phillip, *The Concept of Grace*. Muhlenberg Press, 1959.

CONSERVATISM

Beegle, Dewey M., *The Inspiration of Scripture*. The Westminster Press, 1963.

Carnell, Edward J., *The Case for Orthodox Theology*. The Westminster Press, 1959.

——— *Christian Commitment*. The Macmillan Company, 1957.

—————— *An Introduction to Christian Apologetics.* Eerdmans Publishing Company, 1948.

Machén, John G., *Christianity and Liberalism.* The Macmillan Company, 1923.

—————— *What Is Faith?* The Macmillan Company, 1935.

Tenney, Merrill C., ed., *The Word for This Century.* Oxford University Press, 1960.

LIBERALISM AND NEO-LIBERALISM

De Wolf, L. Harold, *The Case for Theology in Liberal Perspective.* The Westminster Press, 1959.

—————— *A Theology of the Living Church.* Harper & Brothers, 1960.

Fosdick, Harry E., *As I See Religion.* Harper & Brothers, 1932.

—————— *The Man From Nazareth.* Harper & Brothers, 1949.

—————— *Rufus Jones Speaks to Our Time.* The Macmillan Company, 1951.

Harkness, Georgia, *Conflicts in Religious Thought.* Harper & Brothers, 1949.

Van Dusen, Henry P., *The Vindication of Liberal Theology.* Charles Scribner's Sons, 1963.

Williams, Daniel Day, *God's Grace and Man's Hope.* Harper & Brothers, 1949.

NEO-ORTHODOXY

Hordern, William, *The Case for a New Reformation Theology.* The Westminster Press, 1959.

Hubben, William, *Four Prophets of Our Destiny.* The Macmillan Company, 1952.

EMIL BRUNNER

Brunner, Emil, *I Believe in the Living God.* The Westminster Press, 1961.

—————— *Truth as Encounter.* The Westminster Press, 1964.

KARL BARTH

Barth, Karl, *Deliverance to the Captives.* Harper & Brothers, 1961.

――― *Evangelical Theology.* Holt, Rinehart and Winston, 1963.

――― *The Humanity of God.* John Knox Press, 1960.

REINHOLD NIEBUHR

Niebuhr, Reinhold, *The Children of Light and the Children of Darkness.* Charles Scribner's Sons, 1944.

――― *An Interpretation of Christian Ethics.* Harper & Brothers, 1935.

――― *The Self and the Dramas of History.* Charles Scribner's Sons, 1955.

PAUL TILLICH

Tillich, Paul, *Love, Power, and Justice.* Oxford University Press, 1954.

――― *The New Being.* Charles Scribner's Sons, 1955.

――― *The Shaking of the Foundations.* Charles Scribner's Sons, 1948.

RUDOLF BULTMANN

Bultmann, Rudolph, *Jesus Christ and Mythology.* Charles Scribner's Sons, 1958.

――― *This World and Beyond.* Charles Scribner's Sons, 1960.

Bartsch, Hans, *Kerygma and Myth.* S. P. C. K., 1954.

DIETRICH BONHOEFFER

Bonhoeffer, Dietrich, *The Cost of Discipleship.* SCM Press, 1959.

――― *No Rusty Swords.* Harper & Row, 1965.

――― *Prisoner for God.* The Macmillan Company, 1960.

WORLDLY CHRISTIANITY

Callahan, Daniel, ed., *The Secular City Debate.* The Macmillan Company, 1966.

Cox, Harvey, *The Secular City.* The Macmillan Company, 1965.

Gilkey, Langdon, *How the Church Can Minister to the World without Losing Itself.* Harper & Row, 1964.

Jenkins, Daniel, *Beyond Religion.* The Westminster Press, 1962.

Stringfellow, William, *Dissenter in a Great Society.* Holt, Rinehart and Winston, 1966.

———— *My People Is the Enemy.* Holt, Rinehart and Winston, 1964.

Van Buren, Paul, *The Secular Meaning of the Gospel.* The Macmillan Company, 1963.

Williams, Colin, *Faith in a Secular Age.* Collins-Fontana Books, 1966.

———— *Where in the World?* National Council of Churches, 1963.

GOD-IS-DEAD THEOLOGY

Altizer, Thomas J., *The Gospel of Christian Atheism.* The Westminster Press, 1966.

Altizer, Thomas, and Hamilton, William, *Radical Theology and the Death of God.* Bobbs-Merrill, 1966.

Hamilton, Kenneth, *God Is Dead: The Anatomy of a Slogan.* Eerdmans Publishing Company, 1966.

———— *Revolt Against Heaven.* Eerdmans Publishing Company, 1965.

Hamilton, William, *The New Essence of Christianity.* Association Press, 1961.

Ogletree, Thomas, *The Death of God Controversy.* SCM Press, 1966.

Index